SHAKESPEARE'S LANGUAGE

An Introduction

SHAKESPEARE'S LANGUAGE

An Introduction

N. F. BLAKE
Professor of English Language
University of Sheffield

St. Martin's Press New York

St. Martin's Press, Inc., 175 Fifth Avenue, New York, N.Y. 10010
Printed in Hong Kong
First published in the United States of America in 1983

ISBN 0-312-71429-7

Library of Congress Cataloging in Publication Data

Blake, N. F. (Norman Francis)
Shakespeare's language.

Bibliography: p.
Includes index.
1. Shakespeare, William, 1564 – 1616 – Language – Grammar. 2. English language—Early modern, 1500 – 1700. I. Title.
PR3075.B55 1983 822.3'3 82-22995
ISBN 0-312-71429-7

Contents

Preface

This book is not a grammar of Shakespeare's language; and it offers no new interpretation of Shakespeare's plays. It is an introduction to various aspects of the language of Shakespeare and his contemporaries for readers of his plays so that they can more readily understand its structure. It is designed to help readers come to a greater understanding of the language of the time so that they can avoid misinterpretations, recognise the various possibilities of linguistic meaning, and so arrive at a greater depth in their appreciation of Shakespeare's artistry. I have employed a few linguistic terms that are commonly used in modern grammars, but even readers with no formal grammatical training should have little difficulty in coping with the discussions of language. I have tried to avoid using linguistic jargon. Throughout the book I have quoted from the First Folio or occasionally from early quartos where the Folio does not contain the work or the passage in question. I have, however, keyed the quotations to the lineation in the Alexander edition, which is the only complete one readily and cheaply available in England.

While I have been writing this book I have given many lectures based on it to a variety of audiences in diverse parts of England. I am grateful to my audiences for their questions and comments. I am also indebted to my students and my colleagues in the Department of English Language at Sheffield with whom I have had many discussions upon the matters treated here. I should like to offer my particular thanks to Sandra Burton who has prepared the typescript and assisted with the compilation of the index.

SHEFFIELD, DECEMBER 1981

Ye know not, what hurt ye do to learning, that care not for wordes, but for matter.

Roger Ascham, *The Scholemaster*

Abbreviations

Abbreviations of the titles of Shakespeare's plays used in this book are as follows:

Ado	*Much Ado About Nothing*
Ant.	*Antony and Cleopatra*
AW	*All's Well that Ends Well*
AYL	*As You Like It*
Cor.	*Coriolanus*
Cym.	*Cymbeline*
1H4	*The First Part of King Henry the Fourth*
2H4	*The Second Part of King Henry the Fourth*
H5	*King Henry the Fifth*
1H6	*The First Part of King Henry the Sixth*
2H6	*The Second Part of King Henry the Sixth*
3H6	*The Third Part of King Henry the Sixth*
Ham.	*Hamlet*
JC	*Julius Caesar*
John	*King John*
Lear	*King Lear*
LLL	*Love's Labour's Lost*
Macb.	*Macbeth*
Meas.	*Measure for Measure*

Merch.	*The Merchant of Venice*
MND	*A Midsummer Night's Dream*
MWW	*The Merry Wives of Windsor*
Oth.	*Othello*
R2	*King Richard the Second*
R3	*King Richard the Third*
RJ	*Romeo and Juliet*
Shrew	*The Taming of the Shrew*
Temp.	*The Tempest*
TGV	*Two Gentlemen of Verona*
Tim.	*Timon of Athens*
TN	*Twelfth Night*
Troil.	*Troilus and Cressida*
WT	*The Winter's Tale*

Other abbreviations:

OED	*The Oxford English Dictionary*
SS	*Shakespeare Survey*

Introduction

Shakespeare is like food; we take both very much for granted. It is only when we come across a passage of particular intensity in a play that we question how the language has been employed to achieve that result, just as it is only for exotic dishes that we enquire about the ingredients. Most children are introduced to Shakespeare by about the third year at secondary school. From then on he forms a regular part of most school curricula and, of course, new texts are studied at O and A level. In addition visits to the theatre to see Shakespearian productions are arranged by schools and parents. At university a degree in English literature without a course on Shakespeare would seem inconceivable to the average student. To many, therefore, Shakespeare may well seem more familiar than most modern dramatists. This situation is accentuated by the assimilation of so many Shakespearian expressions in our daily language. Most people probably get to know the phrase 'patience on a monument' long before they come across it in *Twelfth Night*; and when they do read or hear it in the play it is like meeting an old friend. The play does not strike one as strange or new. This sense of familiarity encourages students to think they understand the language of Shakespeare's plays, though when they are asked at university to translate a passage it comes as a shock to realise how much is uncertain. This reaction is not entirely their fault. Although there is no shortage of books about Shakespeare's language, they are either arranged as grammars listing all features of his language or they deal with points of special interest to linguists. Students of literature may not understand the terminology of such books and probably assume that the formal ordering of linguistic phenomena is of little help in literary appreciation.

Furthermore, the texts they read at school or university rarely contain an account of Shakespeare's language or a glossary of

Elizabethan words and phrases not found today. Only the occasional word or sentence is explained. The impression is given that provided the odd difficult word is translated, there should be no difficulty in understanding what Shakespeare wrote. There is no suggestion that the way sentences were organised in the Elizabethan period or the effects that could be achieved at that time are different from anything one might find in a modern book.

A few examples may best illustrate that the difficulties involved in reading Shakespeare extend far beyond the question of understanding the literal meaning of a few words or phrases. Sometimes we bring to Shakespearian sentences modern attitudes of correctness and propriety. Few people today are likely to misunderstand 'This was the most vnkindest cut of all' (*JC* III ii 183), though it may appear strange to some. Here 'most vnkindest' is frequently described as a double superlative, for *most* is used as well as the superlative inflexion *-est*. Examples of the comparable double comparative (*cf.* 'To some more fitter place' *Meas.* II ii 17) also occur. The description of such forms as double comparatives and superlatives arises in part because we today confine *more* and *most* largely to the function of comparison. The trend to restrict the range of these words was found already at the end of the seventeenth century, for attacks on this construction as a grammatical mistake begin to appear at that time. As the dictates of logic and Latin grammar made themselves felt with the onset of the so-called Age of Reason, a construction which was apparently repetitive because it used two separate means to achieve one grammatical end naturally came to be considered incorrect. The double superlative further offended logic in that it suggested that there could be degrees in what is superlative, whereas there can logically be only one best or worst of anything. Dryden's criticism of the construction is perhaps best known. In his *Defence of the Epilogue* he attacked Jonson for using it. 'I think few of our present Writers would have left behind them such a line as this:

Contain your Spirit in more stricter bounds.

But that gross way of two Comparatives was then, ordinary: and therefore more pardonable in *Jonson.*' Because Jonson was learned and made such mistakes in correct usage, Dryden expected even less from Shakespeare who lacked Jonson's learning. Pope was equally disturbed by the construction and when he edited Shakespeare's plays he introduced readings which eliminated the double forms. Thus the line from *Julius Caesar* quoted above became 'This, this, was the unkindest cut' and that from *Measure for Measure* was transformed into 'To some more fitting place.' It is possible that the wish to avoid this construction was already felt shortly after Shakespeare's death, for where in *King Lear* the first two quartos read 'Most best, most deerest' (*Lear* I i 216), the Folio reads 'The best, the deerest'. It is followed in this reading by almost all modern editors, who may prefer the Folio reading precisely because it avoids the double superlative. In other words grammatical prejudice may be subconsciously affecting editorial choice.

In approaching these so-called double comparisons we need to remember that *more* and *most* were originally adjectives and adverbs. As the former they had the meaning 'bigger' and 'biggest' in size, and as the latter they were particularly used as intensifiers with the sense 'very, absolutely' used to emphasise the meaning of the following adjective or adverb. Examples from *Hamlet* can exhibit this meaning of the intensifier. In 'Oh horrible, Oh horrible, most horrible' (I v 80) *most* is not used to form the superlative, but for emphasis. It varies and complements the two previous *Oh's* and confirms the terrible nature of the murder. Later when Hamlet drags the body of Polonius from his mother's room, he says that Polonius 'Is now most still, most secret, and most graue' (III iv 214). In this case also there is no question of *most* forming superlatives. Polonius is not now, for example, the quietest person, for he shares his quietness with all other dead persons; he is merely very quiet in death as compared with his garrulity when alive. As it happens intensifiers are among the vogue words of a language which quickly fall out of use as fashions change. Shakespeare himself experiments with them freely. When in the same play the King refers to 'the primall eldest curse' (III iii 37), we may interpret *primall* as a kind of intensifier which comes close to acting as a double superlative meaning little more than 'the very oldest curse'. Yet because Shakespeare has here used *primall eldest* rather than *most eldest*, he is more likely to be praised for inventiveness than criticised for repetition. Similarly in *Hamlet* we find many examples where an adjective or adverb is repeated so that the first acts as an intensifier to the second in a way that is not dissimilar to the double comparisons. The best-known example is 'Oh that this too too solid Flesh, would melt' (I ii 129). Other examples include 'Excellent, excellent well' (II ii 173), 'quite, quite downe' (III i 154), 'A verie verie Paiocke' (III ii 278), and 'those many many bodies' (III iii 9). It is even possible that the Queen's 'Drown'd, drown'd' (IV vii 185) should be interpreted in a similar way.

In fact the wish to emphasise what is already emphatic or superlative and to qualify what might not logically appear to accept qualification is still a feature of modern speech. It is common to come across such utterances as 'quite, quite beautiful', 'the very best', and 'absolutely unique', even if some grammarians might frown on them. Yet even they are hardly likely to object to the modern 'much closer' or even to Shakespeare's 'something neerer' (*WT* II ii 55), though they describe his 'more neerer' (*Ham.* II i 11) as a double comparative and hence imply it is a mistake. The sole difference between today's usage and Elizabethan times is that *more* and *most* are no longer intensifiers. They have been restricted to the formation of comparatives and superlatives precisely because grammarians objected to their double function. It is probably more accurate to describe Shakespearian *more* and *most* as intensifiers when they are used in front of comparatives and superlatives, and that description would help to remove that feeling of unease experienced by most modern readers when faced with these forms.

Modern students react to expressions like *most vnkindest* in one of three ways, all equally misguided. The first is to think Shakespeare knew little grammar as though he were some kind of untutored genius from rural Warwickshire who came to capture the literary heights of London. Such a view is quite false for even if Shakespeare was not among the most educated men of his time, his education was sound enough, and in this particular usage his speech did not differ from that of his most cultivated contemporaries. The second is to assume that he was here flouting the conventions of grammar in order to achieve a special effect. This reaction is understandable today since it is a stance adopted by modern writers like Dylan Thomas who go out of their way to shock. Since grammar is to them a formal constraint, they can shock by flouting the educational conventions characterised by taught grammar. Since Shakespeare lived before the period when English grammar was codified by the grammarians or taught as a subject in schools, he is hardly likely to have felt it as a restraint any more than his contemporaries would have realised that it could be flouted to create a particular effect. The third is to think that in Shakespeare's time there was no grammar and hence that anything was permissible. But all languages at all periods have a grammar, by which one may understand current practice in indicating the relationship between the various parts of the sentence, though not all develop so quickly a formal codified grammar which is used in social and educational circles as a method of accepting certain utterances as correct and others as marks of ill-breeding. There may be more variety in Shakespeare's usage than our own because the grammarians had not by his time dictated what was acceptable, but that variety had limits. It was not possible to go beyond those limits without producing lack of intelligibility. Language has its restrictions, even if they are not always so formalised as the conventions of educational grammars, and those limits need to be appreciated in order to come to terms with the language of any period. If students misunderstand the implications of these forms, scholars also react against them if only subconsciously. As we have seen, it is possible that some editors, when they have a choice, prefer readings which do not involve these forms.

Another misreading of Shakespeare that modern students easily succumb to concerns the stylistic level of particular types of utterance. A typical example is the position of the preposition. It is common in English to place a preposition at the end of a relative clause as in the Authorised Version's 'all this land that I have spoken of' (Exodus 32:13). This type of construction, which is not affected by the particular relative pronoun or even indeed its absence, is found from Old English times onwards and occurs with considerable frequency in Shakespeare, the Bible and Milton. At the end of the seventeenth century the construction came in for criticism because it was felt that a preposition ought, as its name implies, to precede the relative pronoun it governs. This new grammatical norm apparently finds its first expression in Dryden. When he republished his *Essay on Dramatic Poesy* in 1684 he altered all the examples of the final preposition which had occurred in the 1668 edition. Hence 'the age I live in' was altered to 'the age in which I live'. The efforts of the grammarians have not succeeded in eradicating this idiom from the spoken language, though they have had considerable success in making it less frequent in writing. The modern attitude to a final preposition was set by Bishop Lowth who in his influential *Introduction to English Grammar* of 1762 wrote after giving an example: 'This is an idiom, which our language is strongly inclined to: it prevails in common conversation, and suits very well with the familiar style in writing: but the placing of the Preposition before the Relative is more graceful as well as more perspicuous; and agrees much better with the solemn and elevated style.' Consequently many people today still regard the final preposition as either informal or colloquial. It is not surprising therefore that modern students when they come across an example such as Bertram's 'desp'rate creature, Whom sometime I haue laugh'd with' (*AW* V iii 176–7) should assume that Shakespeare was there putting a colloquialism into the mouth of his character. Such a deduction is quite unfounded, for it is based on the presumptions of Modern English rather than of Shakespearian language.

An example which illustrates other aspects of interpretation concerns the second person forms of the personal pronoun. In Modern English the second person has only one form, *you*, which acts as both singular and plural. In earlier English there were separate forms for the singular and plural, *thou* and *you*, though the two had begun to overlap in the Middle English period when *ye/you* forms were extended to the singular. Thus the choice between the two forms became not simply one of number, and there was a trend for *you* to act as the unmarked and *thou* as the marked form in the singular. This means that when *thou* was used it carried more information than simply 'singular', for it was used to indicate familiarity or contempt. In this it resembles French *tu* and German *du* which contrast respectively with *vous* and *Sie*. Because it is not a feature of his own speech, it is easy for the modern reader simply to ignore the implications of the *thou* forms which are more usually just considered the old way of saying 'you'. There can be no doubt, however, that Shakespeare used *thou* in this marked way. When in *Twelfth Night* Sir Toby incites Sir Andrew to be insulting towards the disguised Viola, he says 'if thou thou'st him some thrice, it shall not be amisse' (III ii 41). Kent in *King Lear* was deliberately rude when he addressed the king 'what wouldest thou do old man?' (I i 145). In *The Winter's Tale* Act Three, Scene Two, Paulina first addresses Leontes as *thou* to indicate her contempt for his behaviour, although he is her king. Gradually as Leontes comes to repent of his jealousy towards Hermione, Paulina slips into *you* forms and so re-establishes the distance between herself and her sovereign.

This extra meaning of the marked form of *thou* may occur in unlikely places and so is easily overlooked. In the opening scene of *Hamlet* in which Barnado, Marcellus and Horatio are suddenly confronted with the ghost, the following exchange takes place:

BARN.: It would be spoke too.
MAR.: Question it *Horatio*.
HOR.: What art thou that vsurp'st this time of night,
Together with that Faire and Warlike forme
In which the Maiesty of buried Denmarke
Did sometimes march: By Heauen I charge thee speake.
MAR.: It is offended. (I i 45–50)

The problem here is to understand why the ghost is offended, and modern editors have suggested several reasons. Generally they centre round the word *vsurp'st* which, it is claimed, is used by Horatio because he thinks the ghost is not the spirit of the late king but some devilish impostor who has appropriated his trappings to deceive the Danes. This is a possible explanation, though it is not entirely convincing. The word *usurp* is used commonly with a figurative range of meaning by Shakespeare and other Elizabethan authors. In *Hamlet* we find in the play within a play Lucianus's poison will 'vsurpe immediately' the life of the Player King (III ii 254), and in *Titus Andronicus* sorrow 'would vsurpe vpon my watry eyes' (III i 269). In the passage from the first scene quoted above we would have to assume that the audience realised that *vsurp'st* was here used not metaphorically, but in a significant literal sense. Furthermore attempts to read into the meaning of *usurp* underline a modern approach to literary appreciation, for we today are quick to see nuances in the uses of vocabulary, though this is something which comes more readily through the reflection of silent reading. The predominant position we accord to vocabulary makes us ignore the impact which *thou* had on a contemporary audience.

To Horatio and to the other characters in the play, the ghost is a spirit which is not human. It is therefore referred to as *it* by all speakers and it is not unnatural that they should address it as *thou* which implies a mixture of both contempt and fear. The spirit is, however, the ghost of the former king and still thinks of itself as a king. It is naturally offended when it is addressed in a manner reserved for inferior or contemptible mortals, for it cannot throw off the trappings of royalty so easily. Through a linguistic mechanism Shakespeare is able to indicate that the ghost is indeed the spirit of the old king (for no mere demon would be offended by a *thou*) and that humans naturally approach such spirits with a mixture of superiority and fear. Throughout the play it is addressed by humans in the same way for they continue to use *it* and *thou*, but once the point about its objection to *thou* has been made at the beginning it does not need to be repeated later. The important lesson of this example is that the choice among linguistic items is not the same today as it was in earlier stages of the language. Because we lay such store upon verbal innuendo, we may only too easily overlook the pointers provided by Shakespeare.

A final example may be chosen to exhibit a difference in organisation of the parts of a sentence between the Elizabethan period and our own. In *Hamlet*, when Horatio and the two watchmen tell Hamlet of their encounter with the ghost, the following exchange takes place:

HAM.: His Beard was grisly? no.
HOR.: It was, as I haue seene it in his life,
A Sable Siluer'd. (I ii 239–41)

When I ask my students about the last phrase they generally understand it to mean 'a sable-silver'd (one)'; that is, they assume that some noun or indefinite pronoun is understood and they take the two adjectives to form a compound. This for many of them makes the ghost seem old, for the emphasis falls on the *siluer'd*; and indeed in modern productions he is often represented as grey (though admittedly this could be intended to make him seem more spectral). The reasons for this interpretation on the part of my students are two. It is unusual today to transform an adjective into a noun: a sentence like 'He's an old' is not acceptable. Such forms as do exist in English like 'a penny dreadful' are those hallowed by tradition. In Elizabethan times, however, nouns formed from adjectives are plentiful, and this applies as much to Shakespeare as to any other writer of the time. The ability to employ an adjective in this way introduces the second difficulty for modern speakers, namely which of the two adjectives is to be taken as a noun. In modern descriptions of language we refer to phrases like *a sable siluer'd* as a nominal group, that is a group consisting of one or more words which could act as the subject of a clause. Nominal groups contain a head upon which the other words in the group (where they occur) depend. The words which precede the head are described as modifiers, and in modern English they consist normally of words rather than phrases, and those that follow the head are described as qualifiers, and in modern English they consist of phrases. Hence in modern English it is possible to deduce that the last single word in a nominal group is the head. This is how we can tell that 'a bicycle rally' and 'a rally bicycle' are two different things with 'rally' and 'bicycle' as their respective heads. Whereas it is possible to add a qualifier consisting of a phrase after the head, such as 'a rally bicycle with dropped handlebars', it is not possible to add one consisting of a single word like 'a rally bicycle old'. If a single word does follow 'bicycle' as part of the nominal group, it would by definition be the head of that group as in 'a rally bicycle event', i.e. an event for rally bicycles. Normally single-word qualifiers follow the head in modern English only in traditional expressions like 'little boy blue'.

Such traditional expressions reveal that in the past it was possible to have single-word qualifiers in English and that type of construction is frequent in Shakespeare's writings. Thus in *a sable siluer'd* either *sable* or *siluer'd* could be the head, and modern syntax might encourage us to choose the latter. In fact it is customary to accept that *sable* is the head, for past participial adjectives less frequently underwent a shift from adjective to noun. However, if *sable* is the head, the ghost had a black beard with only a few grey hairs in it. As Horatio says that the beard was the same as he had seen it *in his life*, i.e. when the king was alive, it implies that the king was struck down in the prime of his life. Modern theatrical representations of the king as aged are incorrect and arise from insufficient attention to the text.

In general there was more variety in Elizabethan usage than in our own. Many of the variants have been eliminated in modern standard written English through the normal processes of change in language or through the intervention of grammarians working to the dictates of logic or a Latin-based grammar. Some of the variants thus eliminated have survived colloquially, in dialects or as archaisms, though others have disappeared from the language altogether. Hence to modern readers there is a temptation to interpret such variants with a modern connotation inspired by present-day usage.

Such misunderstandings are accentuated because students of literature are often taught little or nothing about language and how it works. It is accepted that to read literature it is necessary to have some training in the conventions writers use: one has to acquire a literary competence. It is not so readily recognised that the same applies to a linguistic competence, and that to read the literature of the past one has to come to terms with the language of the time. Otherwise one must read past literature as if it were written in modern English with no more than the allowance for the odd archaism. This distant attitude to language is not one shared by the writers themselves, who in the struggle with expression have naturally felt the attraction of language. Many of them chose their particular literary forms of expression partly through their involvement in contemporary linguistic issues. One scholar has written of Hopkins:

> It is important to emphasize that Hopkins was in many ways *part of* this philological movement, displaying the same painstaking care in definition and description of words that was displayed by lexicographers, and the same fascinated interest in the history and relationship of words. . . . In the nineteenth century [philological study] was new, stimulating and full of wonder. Nor is it correct to say that it was Hopkins who breathed life into philology; on the contrary, it was philology that helped to breathe life into Hopkins's poetry.[1]

Writers as diverse as Ben Jonson and Bernard Shaw have succumbed to the fascination of language and the study of language. This is not to deny that many writers have expressed an emotional response to language as though that was the only way to read a work of literature.[2] Such statements may have assisted the separation of language and literary studies, though this can hardly have been the intention of those who wrote them.

The story of how language has been separated from the criticism of literature is a long one and only a few salient points can be referred to here. Until the eighteenth century in England literary figures were accepted as the arbiters of language and style, for their writing embodied the highest expression which English was capable of. Hence it represented a style that all educated people wished to emulate. This desire to imitate the best, which affected prose as much as poetry, is no longer operative: no one today would rush out to buy the poet laureate's latest book to find out how to compose a letter of application for a job, even if it were for one in a department of English in a university. Several reasons have brought this state of affairs about.

In the past the concept of literature was both wider and more unified than it is today. It included anything which might be said to rise above the merely utilitarian: sermons, biographies, diaries, histories, poems and even polemical works. Indeed anything that fell in the *belles lettres* tradition was accepted as literature. This wide-ranging concept was undermined first by the separation of poetry and prose, both of which had been regarded previously as suitable media for literary expression. The growth in the output of prose, which was naturally a growth in expressing more mundane affairs, has made it seem the appropriate medium for ordinary, non-literary writings. Few prose works are today considered as literature, though almost all poetry is. This separation commenced in the eighteenth century and it has become more marked since then as poetry has concentrated its energies more towards the short lyric of intense emotion and left prose to do everything else. The multifarious purposes for which prose is now used have contaminated its role as a literary medium.

In pre-nineteenth-century England the writer, whether poet or prose writer, was a craftsman who perfected his abilities through imitation of the approved models. Through this imitation he was introduced to what was best in the language and so came to emulate and then to improve on his teachers. The Romantic Revolution put a different emphasis on literary work. Originality and sincerity became more valued than poetic craftsmanship. New claims were made for the poet and his role in society: he ceased to be the arbiter of language, but he became the seer of great emotional intensity whose job it was to educate others into the higher reaches of sensitive awareness to the world. Lyrical poetry became more popular because in it originality and sincerity are more readily preserved. This attitude has led incidentally to the undervaluing of those periods of English literature in which the long poem predominates, such as the fifteenth century, because long poems will rarely exhibit these features to a great degree. This change has not, however, been an unmixed blessing. It has created a language problem for the individual poet. For him to rely too much on the past in his language might smack of lack of originality; but to go in for one's own language may easily result in obscurity. From the nineteenth century onwards each poet has been faced with the problem of what is known as 'finding his voice'. He has to choose those elements from the past and from the present which suit his message and he has to weld them into a suitable literary and linguistic vehicle. Some poets have veered more to archaism; others to colloquialism; and yet others to dislocation of the language. There is no longer a unified poetic language which poets can adopt and which contemporary readers can understand and identify with. The greater the insecurity of its linguistic foundations, the more esoteric poetry became. Today each poet uses an individual and special form of language; and there is a temptation to assume that this has always been so.

This change took place against new attitudes towards the teaching of English. It was the absence of formal instruction in English grammar which perhaps allowed older writers to be taken as models of style. This want was gradually supplied in the eighteenth and nineteenth centuries and it was associated with a growing sense of correctness in language. This development produced professional language men who set themselves up as the judges of correctness. At first in the eighteenth century it was possible to combine the role of grammarian with that of literary writer, as Dr Johnson did, but gradually the two professions recruited separate individuals to their ranks. With the growing interest in grammar there was a tendency to assume that correctness was the most important feature in language – more important even than literary expression. This tendency drove a wedge between grammar and style, for to many it might seem that felicity of expression should be measured in terms of correctness. As we have seen, Dryden objected to Elizabethan style precisely because it was incorrect.

The twentieth century has witnessed the growth of university departments of English. At first the uncertainty about modern literature and how to teach it led English departments to adopt a historical approach to literature with a large amount of language and medieval work, which included mastering some of the techniques of language. In Cambridge this development was less marked because the medieval branches of English were grouped more closely with archaeology than with literature. There the reaction against language in literary studies matured earliest and with it went the demand to teach 'literature as literature'. This demand reflected the growing confidence of teachers of literature in their own subject which resulted in their making greater claims for it. To some these claims involved the freeing of literary criticism from the restraints of language and history which were seen as inhibiting aspects. In this approach teachers of literature joined hands with the new emotionalism associated with the Romantic Revolution and the new professionalism of criticism developed in America under the banner of the New Criticism. For New Criticism has insisted on looking at any piece of literature in isolation without any built-in assumptions.

Writing had to make its appeal directly without the confusing intermediaries of the study of language, history or biography, for this was the only way it could make an immediate emotional impact.

This new philosophy has produced that favourite modern literary exercise of practical criticism, which in its purest form invites a student to respond to a passage of literature without knowing its date, author or critical standing. As an exercise it has certain disadvantages. It is not possible for a student presented with such an 'anonymous' passage to approach it historically or to try to understand its language against the language environment in which it was written. Consequently each passage tends to be read as though it was a modern composition, for a student is most influenced by the literary fashions of his own age. Hence passages which have linguistic or historical complexities tend to be avoided in practical criticism, though such an avoidance suggests there is something fundamentally wrong with the philosophy of the exercise. Equally practical criticism encourages students to look for literary sophistication and linguistic innuendo in texts of any period, since these are the favoured responses to modern literature. Such a search has naturally to be conducted in a quite anachronistic way.

Paradoxically the divorce between language and literature may have grown as a result of the development of linguistic studies as a separate discipline in universities. Linguistics has absorbed the energies of many language teachers who have become more interested in theoretical approaches to language and the study of spoken varieties of English than in the analysis of historical English. The theoretical concerns of linguistics have often seemed too remote from literature and its jargon too intimidating for critics to attempt to apply its insights to literary criticism. On the Continent this has not been the case where the structural approach to language has been widely adopted by critics as a critical tool. Continental attitudes have begun to have some influence in England, though there is still among critics a considerable distrust of a linguistic approach.[3] After all the anti-historical approach of linguists has led many to think that language study has nothing to offer literary history as though writing was the preserve of literary critics and speech that of linguists. The historical study of language has been ignored by both sides, and in England at least it has found little favour in the post-war period.

These developments have not been without their problems for literary critics. The claim to teach 'literature as literature' encouraged many to suppose that after one has stripped away the language, the historical background, the biography and other peripheral features from a text, there is something left which is 'literature'. This is, of course, quite absurd, for in the process the work itself disappears. What in fact has happened is that as the study of the language and of the historical background has diminished, its place has been taken by thematic approaches to literature. Each work has been subjected to a succession of new readings which in their increasing abstractness leave the surface texture of the work (and thus its language) further behind.[4] Or else older texts are given a Marxist or sociological interpretation, for the thematic approach allows literature to be subjected to a succession of philosophical approaches in which the text itself is virtually ignored. To the chagrin of literary critics the expulsion of language and history from the citadel of literature has permitted the infiltration of what is considered by many of them a more insidious enemy. Literary criticism is too delicate to exist as an independent discipline. If it does not rest upon the foundations of language and history, it has to find other foundations upon which to construct its edifice. One purpose of this book is to suggest that a study of language remains an essential foundation for understanding literature. With a writer from the past this will include having some grasp of the language of his time in order to read his works fully.

1 Language Environment

It is frequently claimed that Shakespeare was fortunate to live at the time he did because English was then both fluid and rich. However, this view should not be over-emphasised since it implies that he would not have become such a master of expressive English if he had lived at any other period. We should remember that there were many bad writers among his contemporaries; the age did not turn bad poets into good ones, though the language may have helped the better ones to be more expressive. Each writer of whatever period has to use the resources of the language of his time and to exploit them to his own purposes. As we shall see, Shakespeare did not exploit all features of his own contemporary language, and it is as instructive to consider what he neglected as what he developed. The linguistic environment a writer can exploit consists of the structure of his language, which in English as in other languages is continually changing, and of the attitudes that his contemporaries have towards their language. Language is a social and cultural phenomenon which is peculiarly influenced by the regard in which it is held, for those who are dissatisfied with its range of expressiveness will embark on what may be called 'linguistic engineering'. They will attempt to correct the faults they detect in their language. The comments of contemporaries reveal what people of the time were concerned about and therefore indicate some of the pressures to which Shakespeare responded.

The Renaissance period is richer than any preceding one in English in the amount and diversity of written material produced. A flood of books came off the presses written in a standardised form of English, though that standard tolerated far more variety than our own. A large amount of informal writing also survives which enables us to gain some insight into regional and social varieties.

Nevertheless, a nation's attitude to its language is coloured by that used in what is considered the best literature rather than by the variety found at different levels. For Renaissance Englishmen the best meant the literature written in a high style. Although we today look back to the Elizabethan period as one of linguistic richness and exuberance, those who lived then viewed things differently. This difference arises because we compare Elizabethan literature with our own to the detriment of the latter. They for their part compared their literature with classical works in Latin and Greek and arrived at the same unfavourable conclusion about their own literature. Writers who have to wrestle with language to express their meaning are prone to feel there are richer possibilities for expression inherent in other periods or languages. It is hardly surprising that each age should contain its laments about the state of contemporary language and its inability to express the highest emotional states. This is true even for Shakespeare and his contemporaries.

One reason for this state of affairs in the Elizabethan period was the rise of humanism, which brought with it a new interest in the classics in their original language and form. Scholars searched for the best manuscripts of famous classical authors and published them so that many texts became available in their original language and shape; they were no longer disguised in medieval adaptations. Schools and universities started to teach classical rather than vulgar Latin, and learned controversies about such erudite matters as the correct pronunciation of classical Latin arose. What is important with respect to English is that classical Latin reappeared as a serious language with a magnificent literature: the past became distanced from the present and so could be held up as a model for emulation. In the language environment the effect was to depress men's regard for their own languages. Classical Latin was a dead language in which only outstanding literary works had survived; these were regarded as the highest form of human expression and were used as models for writing in schools and universities. Latin as a language was permanently excellent: it could not be weakened because no new classical literature could be produced, and it could not be defiled by contact with everyday speech and commerce because it was not a spoken language. English literature and language could not compete with Latin. A tradition of criticising the imperfections of English became established, in which the absence of ornate phraseology, rhetorical excellence and a rich vocabulary is a recurring feature.

The assumed poverty of vocabulary in English arose partly because there was no agreement on how the vocabulary should be expanded to meet the needs of the new discoveries in science and geography and to provide the variety of words needed for rhetorical elaboration. As a Germanic language, English had formerly created new words through compounding, as German still does. The Norman Conquest had encouraged the importation of foreign words mostly of Latin origin, though such words could hardly seem as natural or intelligible in English as they were in French. English thus occupied an intermediate position between Germanic word-compounding on the one hand and neologisms of Latin-based words on the other. It was not surprising that this situation should lead to controversy as to the best way to enlarge the wordstock, in which the only point the contestants were agreed upon was the need for the enlargement because of the contemporary language's inadequacy. The greater expressiveness and richness of the languages from which the loan-words came was claimed to be the advantage of borrowing classical words, as though that expressiveness and richness would somehow be transferred to English. The disadvantage was that in a period of burgeoning knowledge so many foreign words are imported that not only will the language be in danger of losing its character, but also the sheer influx of foreign words could hinder rather than assist intelligibility.

It is not necessary to accept these criticisms of the poverty of English any more than one need believe the jeremiads about the modern language which appear today with such regularity in some newspapers. It is, however, important to know that these criticisms were made in order to appreciate that writers were conscious of the need to elevate the language. Since the end of the seventeenth century the normal reaction to any call to improve the language has been to inculcate standards of correctness. Even recently in the so-called Great Debate on education, which considered the 'problem' of English and its impoverishment, a favourite proposal was that children should once again be taught to spell, punctuate and phrase their utterances correctly. This solution was not available in the sixteenth and early seventeenth century because standards of correctness had not then evolved. That standards had not evolved is attributable to humanism which concentrated men's minds on Latin and the need to make it a suitable vehicle for instruction by explaining its grammar and deciding its pronunciation. There was no time to tackle English in the same way. Hence in the Elizabethan period there was an intense interest in language, though as far as grammar is concerned that interest was directed at languages other than English. Improvements in eloquence and richness could not be provided by correctness. So eloquence was supplied by rhetoric and richness by lexical invention.

Rhetoric, that is the rules followed by writers to assist them to write persuasively and elegantly, was not a creation of the sixteenth century. Rhetorical manuals which contained the rules of writing had been written since the twelfth century, though they were in Latin and were designed as aids to the composition of Latin. Chaucer and fifteenth-century English writers had adopted many of the recommendations of these handbooks in their poems. The sixteenth century witnessed the writing of rhetorical handbooks in English as an aid for English authors, of which Puttenham's *The Arte of English Poesie* (1589) and Fraunce's *Arcadian Rhetoric* (1588) are among the best known. In addition to other matter these books contain lists of rhetorical figures with examples in English or Latin. It is not necessary to give a list of such figures here. For the most part they consist of figures of sound or figures of sense, in both of which the language is manipulated to produce particular effects. The aim of rhetoric is artificial and literary; and it is important to bear this in mind when dealing with a dramatist like Shakespeare in whose work modern readers expect to find the adaptation of language to individual characters in a naturalistic way. In this period the most approved language was that which was most artificial; it was not that which approximated most closely to realism of speech or colloquialism. At the same time rhetorical precepts embodied an approach to language which was shared by all people of the time: it was a known and approved convention. People would look for it and respond to it. It enabled the writers to share a community of outlook and approach with their audience.

Two forms of verbal enrichment need to be considered as part of the attempt to improve the language. The first is that of enlarging the wordstock principally through foreign loanwords. The formation of new compounds from words already in the language was also prompted by foreign models. The use of compounds in Spenser's poetry is an imitation of French models, particularly that of du Bartas. This desire to enrich the language through introducing new words may have encouraged the many translations which were made at this time, for in them many of the original words were kept even though they were given an English dress. There can be no doubt that the spirit of the age encouraged innovation in vocabulary for its own sake, and in all forms of literature this went beyond the strictly necessary or utilitarian. Poets and dramatists vied with one another to see who could introduce the most obscure and high-sounding words. Rhetoric was equated with ornate vocabulary rather than with appropriateness of expression so that there was no reconciliation between words and matter. As Thomas Wilson put it in his *Arte of Rhetorique* 'hee that can catche an ynke horne terme by the taile, hym thei coumpt to be a fine Englisheman, and a good *Rhetorician.*' In this art Shakespeare was regarded as a pastmaster by his contemporaries as is revealed by Robert Green's sneering remark about the young Shakespeare as the 'upstart Crow, beautified with our feathers', who was 'as well able to bumbast out a blanke verse as the best of you.' If his contemporaries regarded Shakespeare as competing in the art of hyperbole, this may be how Shakespeare saw much of his own work.

The second method of verbal enrichment in this period is the use of a whole range of verbal wordplay including punning. Many modern writers think of this as a feature of Elizabethan drama which was introduced as a means of indicating certain colloquial and informal levels of speech. It is more reasonable, however, to regard it as an expression of the reaction to the poverty of English. A feature of this wordplay is its sudden emergence in the Elizabethan period and its rapid decline before the middle of the succeeding century. Punning is as rarely found in medieval drama as in the poems and prose works of late Middle English writers like Chaucer and Gower. When wordplay is introduced into English in a large way, it is found not only in drama but also in all other forms of composition. Then by the middle of the seventeenth century the fashion for verbal play came to an end because of the new attitude to language which developed at that time. Propriety and naturalness of expression were valued and correctness was considered a more appropriate method than verbal wordplay to improve the language. The language was rich enough not to need the support of wordplay any more. Hence punning and other verbal excesses came under increasing condemnation as the century progressed. It therefore seems probable that the explosion in punning and other forms of wordplay in Elizabethan literature is part of the attempt to show that English could be used as expressively as any other language; they represent another aspect of the potential range of English. The growth in wordplay parallels that of new words and there can be little doubt that both arose through the same causes. There was thus in the use of punning an element of showing off, and this applies as much to Shakespeare as to any other writer of the time. These features were not introduced to give naturalness to speech or to represent a particular form of social speech.

In this chapter and the Introduction I have had occasion to refer to the new attitudes to grammar which developed in the middle of the seventeenth century, and this may have left some readers with the impression that the Elizabethan period had no philosophy of grammar or interest in language study. This is not the case, but its interests differed very sharply from those of succeeding centuries. Whereas in later periods correctness in syntax and propriety in vocabulary were the primary concerns, the Elizabethans were more interested in the relationship between sound and writing. The focus of linguistic interest at this period was directed towards sound, not to vocabulary or syntax. This interest is reflected in the controversy over the correct pronunciation of classical Latin to which I have already referred. Writers on the English language show their concern for sound by producing a spate of books on spelling. Richard Mulcaster in his *First Part of the Elementarie* (1582) discussed whether one should spell in accordance with etymology or in accordance with current pronunciation. He came down in favour of ordinary usage, though this raised the problem of how that pronunciation was best represented in writing. Reformers were not slow to propose new alphabets. John Hart is typical of this type of linguist. A competent phonetician, he devised a phonetic writing system which he felt would be suitable to represent English sounds and in his *Orthographie* (1569) he printed examples of English written in this alphabet. Others like William Bullokar, whose new alphabet was published in 1580, produced their own answers to this problem. Shakespeare was clearly influenced by these proposals for he satirises spelling pronunciations in *Love's Labour's Lost* where the pedant Holofernes insists that in *debt* all four letters should be sounded. Unfortunately the alphabets put forward by the reformers differed so much from contemporary spelling habits that they had little chance of being accepted generally; and none of them won the influential support among the aristocracy which was essential if changes were to be adopted. Be that as it may, their proposals show that there was a profound interest in sound at this time. Much educational training, in both universities and schools, was merely verbal, and academic distinction was achieved by proficiency in formal disputation. In 1580 Sir Philip Sidney warned his brother that teaching in Oxford concentrated too much on words to the neglect of things.

If we interpret Shakespeare's language against this background we notice immediately that criticisms through language in the plays invariably involve affectation and hyperbole. The desire to enrich the language led many to go too far and the resulting excess became an obvious target for satire and unfavourable comment. It is part of the temper of the age that this is so. One aspect of this excess is malapropism, which is the abuse for the most part of Latinate words which are by nature of their origin more learned and abstruse than native vocabulary so that many speakers do not know how to pronounce them or what their real meaning is. This type of corruption is met with most frequently among lower-class speakers, but it may perhaps be left on one side now so that it can be considered with wordplay.

More significant are those examples in which more socially elevated people try to use the embellishments of rhetoric in an attempt to cut a figure. Polonius claims that he is 'brief' in his speech, but yet he spins out what he has to say by clothing it in rhetorical adornments. Consider the following passage:

> POL.: Your Noble Sonne is mad:
> Mad call I it; for to define true Madnesse,
> What is't, but to be nothing else but mad.
> But let that go.
> QU.: More matter, with lesse Art.
> POL.: Madam, I sweare I vse no Art at all:
> That he is mad, 'tis true: 'Tis true 'tis pittie,
> And pittie it is true: A foolish figure,
> But farewell it: for I will vse no Art. (II ii 92–9)

The figures he uses here include repeating a word with different endings as in *mad* and *madness* (polyptoton) and repeating a phrase with the order of the principal words reversed as in *'Tis true 'tis pittie, And pittie it is true* (antimetabole). In this instance the rebuke from the Queen, a character not much given to criticism, and the disclaimer by Polonius which serves to call attention to his use of rhetoric imply disapproval by Shakespeare. Rhetoric is here inappropriate, for

Polonius is giving information and opinions, and rhetoric may detract from the intelligibility of what he says. A similar criticism is made of Osricke, the courtier, though part of the scene (V ii) in which he appears is not found in the Folio, which may indicate that the editors found the humour too laboured. In this scene Osricke is sent by the King to propose to Hamlet a duel with Laertes. He uses such hyperbole to deliver the challenge that Hamlet mocks him by going one better:

> COUR.: Nay good my Lord for my ease in good faith, sir here is newly com to Court *Laertes*, belieue me an absolute gentlemen, ful of most excellent differences, of very soft society, and great showing: indeede to speake fellingly of him, hee is the card or kalender of gentry: for you shall find in him the continent of what part a Gentleman would see.
>
> HAM.: Sir, his definement suffers no perdition in you, though I know to deuide him inuentorially, would dazzie th'arithmaticke of memory, and yet but raw neither, in respect of his quick saile, but in the veritie of extolment, I take him to be a soule of great article, & his infusion of such dearth and rarenesse, as to make true dixion of him, his semblable is his mirrour, & who els would trace him, his vmbrage, nothing more. (V ii 105–19, Q²)

Hamlet's speech is sufficient comment on Osricke's manner of talking. It renders Osricke almost speechless, or as Horatio says 'all's golden words are spent'.

An interesting case in *Hamlet* occurs when Polonius reads to the King and Queen Hamlet's letter to Ophelia. This consists of a verse with some of Hamlet's own comments:

> *Doubt thou, the Starres are fire,*
> *Doubt, that the Sunne doth moue,*
> *Doubt Truth to be a Lier,*
> *But neuer Doubt, I loue.*
>
> *O deere Ophelia, I am ill at these Numbers: I haue not Art to reckon my grones; but that I loue thee best, oh most Best beleeue it.* (II ii 115–21)

In this verse the use of anaphora with each line beginning with *Doubt* is noteworthy. Hamlet's own disclaimer seems to suggest that the rhetorical embellishments so characteristic of love lyrics of the

Elizabethan period cannot express the depth and strength of his love.

A less straightforward case is provided by the language of the players. When they perform the play about the murder of Gonzago, the language they use is stilted. The Player King opens the play with these words:

> Full thirtie times hath Phoebus Cart gon round,
> Neptunes salt Wash, and *Tellus* orbed ground:
> And thirtie dozen Moones with borrowed sheene,
> About the World haue times twelue thirties beene,
> Since loue our hearts, and *Hymen* did our hands
> Vnite comutuall, in most sacred Bands. (III ii 150–5)

Here the use of Greek mythology produces circumlocutions for the sun, the sea and the earth. The longwinded nature of these circumlocutions is accentuated by such phrases as *salt Wash.* The first couplet is balanced against the second, and the fifth line is balanced within itself. The repetition of thirty seems somewhat laboured. No comment is made on the language of this play in the outer framework of the main play, and it may be that Shakespeare intended just to differentiate the language of the two plays to keep them apart rather than to criticise one of them. Indeed when the players first appear, Hamlet reminds them that they once performed a play which was '*Cauiarie* to the Generall' and which was 'well digested in the Scœnes, set downe with as much modestie, as cunning' (II ii 430–3). Hamlet says further that he particularly liked a speech, which he then quotes from memory. This speech shows many of the same rhetorical features found in the play about the murder of Gonzago. It is clear that the boundary between acceptable and unacceptable rhetoric is ill-defined.

Hamlet's approval of the players' speech reminds us that both he and other characters use rhetoric freely themselves and sometimes they come close to abusing it. When Laertes and Hamlet have both jumped into Ophelia's grave, Hamlet speaks like this:

> Come show me what thou'lt doe.
> Woo't weepe? Woo't fight? woo't teare thy selfe?
> Woo't drinke vp *Esile*, eate a Crocodile?
> Ile doo't. Dost thou come heere to whine;

To outface me with leaping in her Graue?
Be buried quicke with her, and so will I. (V i 268–73)

Here the repetition of *woo't* and the rhetorical questions are two figures found frequently in contemporary literature, and the whole speech is characterised by exuberance and exaggeration. We must understand that this rhetoric is to be taken seriously here for it reflects Hamlet's passionate feelings, though in the following scene he apologises to Laertes for his behaviour and one may feel that he intended his language to be included in that apology. However, both Hamlet and other characters continue to decorate their language with rhetoric, as indeed they could hardly avoid doing since rhetoric was the means whereby language was arranged in pleasing patterns and telling effects. It was essential in blank verse to indicate which words were stressed and how the language was organised to create a counterpoint to the metre. When rhetoric is not present, it may be difficult to decide whether the words are in prose or verse; and indeed the early quartos and Folio differ over the status of many passages.

The implication is that Shakespeare was sufficiently of his time to use rhetoric (indeed some plays like *Antony and Cleopatra* are notably hyperbolic), though he was very conscious how easily it could be abused. He did not set out to imitate such writers as Marlowe who revelled in the force of swelling bombast. He was aware of the tradition of verbal display and of its excesses; and he tried to avoid the latter. In *The First Part of King Henry the Fourth* he lets Falstaff parody contemporary bombastic style when he says 'for I must speake in passion, and I will doe it in King *Cambyses* vaine' (II iv 375–6). Falstaff then goes on to give some examples of this *vaine*, and no doubt the audience applauded the parody. Similarly in *King Henry the Fifth* Pistol's language is largely made up of echoes and quotations from contemporary writers and dramatists, and one can only conclude that their appearance in the mouth of this braggart was meant as a criticism of the style. This balancing trick between the use of rhetorical figures and the criticism of its excess makes Shakespeare's language difficult to understand, because today it is sometimes impossible to know what tone is being adopted. In general one may follow the simple rule that if the language is not criticised by characters within the play, whether implicitly or explicitly, and if the character is not presented as a braggart or buffoon, the rhetorical conventions were meant to be taken at face value. Shakespeare uses the figures moderately in order to achieve a sense of moderation. This applies equally to his choice of vocabulary. He could exploit Latinate words in English as he does in such phrases as 'The multitudinous Seas incarnardine' (*Macb.* II ii 62). How could a poet as sensitive to the sound of words as he was avoid them? But he can also criticise the mindless adoption of Latin words as he does when Don Adriano refers to 'afternoon' as the 'posteriors of this day' (*LLL* V i 78) and when other characters indulge in malapropisms. Shakespeare is not a learned poet who wants to parade his learning. Latin words are not used for mere exhibition and there are few Latin tags or learned allusions. In this his work differs conspicuously from that of a dramatist like Ben Jonson.

Wordplay has many uses. One of the most common is to pass the time pleasurably when there is no essential dramatic business on hand or no information which needs to be conveyed to the audience. It enlivens many bridge passages. Consequently it is frequently found on the lips of the low-class characters, because their role is often less necessary to the unfolding of the main action which engrosses the attention of the socially elevated people. Yet even they, especially in the comedies, appear in many scenes in which they must while away time without doing much that is dramatic or positive. Thus Beatrice and Benedick in *Much Ado about Nothing* engage in many passages of wit, and the courtiers in *Love's Labour's Lost* do the same. Mercutio and his friends in *Romeo and Juliet* while away the time in this way to the delight of the audience, though Mercutio's own wordplay takes on a more sombre tone at his death. Indeed the wordplay of the courtiers is employed not merely to use up stage-time; it can have a more significant role in pointing to important ideas and themes in the plays. Hamlet's 'A little more then kin, and lesse then kinde' (I ii 65) with its play on *kin* and *kinde* which has almost a proverbial expressiveness sets the tone for Hamlet's language and introduces the themes of natural and unnatural relationships. Wordplay can be comic or serious, high or low class.

Puns may be either homophonic or semantic. The former involves words which sounded alike in at least one variant form in the London speech of the Elizabethan period, for the dramatists frequently drew upon less common pronunciations to achieve their wordplay. As the pronunciation of these words may be different in the modern standard language, it is often difficult for a modern reader or listener to grasp that a pun is involved, particularly if the pun is encapsulated in one word rather than two. Only a specialist in the history of English is likely to know that the *oi* in some words borrowed from French and the *ī* of English words sounded sufficiently alike in the sixteenth and seventeenth centuries for them to be treated as identical sounds. A modern audience would certainly make little of the clause 'let me be boyl'd to death with Melancholly' (*TN* II v 3), although it contains a play on *boil* and *bile*, which like melancholy was one of the four humours. Melancholy was the cold humour, however, - and hence the joke. A semantic pun involves words which have two meanings, one of which is often obscene. The latter may not be familiar today, for each age develops its own bawdy vocabulary, and so the double entendre is easily overlooked. When Gratiano in *The Merchant of Venice* threatens that he will 'mar the yong Clarks pen' (V i 237) if Narissa marries him, many modern listeners and readers may not recognise that *pen* has the second meaning 'penis'.

These types of wordplay exploit for the most part the resources of native words in the language or of foreign words that had been in the language for a long time. It is for this reason that they are not apparent to modern readers, for in the history of the language the original sounds and alternative meanings have become altered. Malapropism on the other hand tends to exploit the more learned and polysyllabic words in the language, and these were often in Elizabethan times of recent foreign origin. Naturally it is such words which are most likely to be misunderstood by those who are less educated. Malapropism usually involves the mispronunciation of some part of the word, particularly the prefixes and suffixes, or the misapplication of the word in a ludicrous context. Malapropism is readily understood today because the language has kept most of the Latinate words, their pronunciation has changed less than that of the native words because of their learned origin, and their corruption can as readily be detected by a modern audience as by an Elizabethan one. That this is so may lead to a faulty appreciation of Shakespeare's art today. Malapropism partakes to some extent of the nature of slapstick, as is true of Dogberry for instance, whereas punning and other forms of wordplay are more subtle. The former is played for laughs in modern productions, but the latter may be ignored. Hence Shakespeare may be understood today by some more as a comic slapstick writer rather than as a dramatist of wit. It is the latter which would have made most impression on his contemporaries.

The inability of a modern audience to understand much of the wit in a Shakespeare play can also lead to a different kind of misunderstanding. Some Elizabethan plays are patently obscene, because they use more explicit vocabulary or are set in brothels and suchlike locations. Shakespeare uses obscenity only in a covert way. Because so much of this covert obscenity is not apparent to modern readers, Shakespeare often seems to them to be different in kind from his contemporaries. It often comes as a shock to many people when they realise how obscene Shakespeare can be, for they had regarded him as 'safe'. If Shakespeare differs from his contemporaries, it is not in the use of obscenity, it is in its expression. Furthermore, wordplay and rhetoric share an important characteristic which is that they put sound before sense. By this I mean that surface grammaticality and logic may be sacrificed in the interests of making a particular effect in which sound is important. Today we are not so ready to pay attention to such sound effects and so editors may try to make more sense out of the surface language than Shakespeare did. Sometimes indeed it is very difficult for an editor to know whether to emend or not. In Sonnet 12 line 4 the Quarto reads 'And sable curls or siluer'd ore with white'. Many editors have decided that this line makes no sense grammatically and so they have emended. The usual solution has been to emend *or* to *all* or *and.* These emendations certainly make the line more acceptable grammatically, but they also destroy the echo between *or* and *ore,* which may have been intended as a wordplay by Shakespeare. He does elsewhere use *or* where no alternative is implied. It may then be interpreted as 'and' as in *Venus and Adonis* 1.10): 'More white, and red, then doues, or roses are.' In *Timon of Athens* (II ii 156), on the other hand, the *or* of 'If you suspect my Husbandry or Falshood' may be interpreted as a kind of hendiadys meaning 'of falsehood in my management'. It may be that in Sonnet 12/4 an explanation along one of these lines should be preferred to emendation so that the wordplay is retained, though it may be admitted that the *or* could be some kind of compositorial mistake. However, the example does underline a point which will recur later in this book: words may not make surface grammatical sense in Shakespeare's works because he often preferred to develop a witty sound effect since at that time such effects were more admired than grammatical logic. This preference can naturally make it difficult to understand some passages, particularly if we insist that every sentence must make perfect grammatical and logical sense at the surface level.

2 Varieties

In the last chapter we saw that Shakespeare's response to the prevailing linguistic attitudes was to indulge in linguistic expressiveness involving wit and sound, and it it possible that these aspects of language were more important to him than the moulding of language to suit the requirements of individual characters. In his plays he used rather a narrow range of the linguistic possibilities of the English of his time so that it is sometimes difficult to identify from a given passage who the speaker is, for few characters in his works have idiosyncrasies which mark them out from all others. Even if a character like Dogberry uses malapropism, his malapropisms are no different in kind from those used by others. Some scholars have tried to isolate certain features of syntax as characteristic of particular characters or even whole plays, such as the interrogatives in *King Richard the Second* and the conditionals used particularly by Falstaff in *The First Part of King Henry the Fourth.*[1] However, in such plays those syntactic features are simply found more frequently than in the other plays and can be detected only through comparison of large stretches of text. Such differences are more subtle than marked features of vocabulary or dialect and can readily be overlooked, particularly in the theatre.

The primary difference in the language of the plays is that between prose and verse. This distinction often represents a social as well as a dramatic contrast, for prose is frequently used by lower-class speakers and for comedy and parody, whereas verse is more characteristic of the socially elevated people who are given to different kinds of rhetorical embellishment. However, this contrast should not be pushed too far, since there are considerable variations within both prose and verse and since each could be used in situations where one might have expected the other. Osricke in *Hamlet* uses prose to deliver his messages and yet he is able to decorate his language in an extravagantly courtly way. Falstaff in *The First Part of King Henry the Fourth* can use prose to imitate the euphuistic and biblical varieties current at the time, and both these forms employed a lot of rhetorical decoration.

Nevertheless, because prose is frequently used to signal comedy, it is found in informal situations and it is employed by low-class people, whose role it often is to provide comic relief in the plays. Hence it has been claimed that the language of the prose is more colloquial and less artificial than that found in the verse. Although there is an element of truth in this claim, it depends very much on what is meant by colloquial, and in general it does less than justice to Shakespeare's artistic use of prose. When low-class characters speak there is little in their language that is necessarily colloquial, as that word would be understood in modern descriptions of language. The absence of elevation and embellishment is not the same thing as colloquialism, though we tend to make such an assumption. Furthermore, we have little knowledge of what colloquialism was like at that time, for the only sources that survive are largely literary or formal. Because of the prevalent convention of naturalism in modern drama we tend to assume that Shakespeare would also have aimed for natural colloquialism in his plays. Quite apart from the artificial conventions of language in the Elizabethan period, Shakespeare's language was less colloquial than that of many contemporaries. 'Shakespeare was in no danger of becoming too colloquial in his dialogue. Even his apparently colloquial prose is a good deal further from actual Elizabethan speech than the dialogue of Middleton or Jonson.'[2]

Let us consider as an example of prose Launcelot Gobbo's opening words in *The Merchant of Venice*:

> Certainely, my conscience will serue me to run from this Iew my Maister: the fiend is at mine elbow, and tempts me, saying to me, *Iobbe*, *Launcelet Iobbe*, good *Launcelet*, or good *Iobbe*, or good *Launcelet Iobbe*, vse your legs, take the start, run awaie: my conscience saies no; take heede honest *Launcelet*, take heed honest *Iobbe*, or as aforesaid honest *Launcelet Iobbe*, doe not runne, scorne running with thy heeles; well, the most coragious fiend bids me packe, *fia* saies the fiend, away saies the fiend, for the heauens rouse vp a braue minde saies the fiend, and run; well, my conscience hanging about the necke of my heart, saies verie wisely to me: my honest friend *Launcelet*, being an honest mans sonne, or rather an honest womans

> sonne, for indeede my Father did something smack, something grow too; he had a kinde of taste; wel, my conscience saies *Launcelet* bouge not.
> (II ii 1–17)

Here there is little or nothing in the vocabulary that has been inserted as a marker of informal language. An expression like *bids me packe* is not colloquial in intention, for the verb *pack* is found elsewhere on the lips of many more elevated speakers. The same is true of *bouge* 'budge'. On the other hand, Launcelot uses more learned words like *afore-said* and literary expressions like *the necke of my heart* which one would not expect to find within a colloquial register. There are no slang, cant or dialect words or forms, unless *fia* is taken to be a dialect or ignorant pronunciation of *via*, the Italian for 'away' – the play being set in Venice and elsewhere in Italy. There are also no contractions or unusual morphological forms, which might be interpreted as signs of lack of education. There are apparent confusions in the logic of the argument in that Launcelot starts by saying his conscience will allow him to run away, but clearly in the passage his conscience counsels against such a course of action. This illogicality has nothing to do with language. On the contrary, the speech is organised in a literary way with repetition, itself a common feature of rhetorical ornament, used extensively as in *vse your legs, take the start, run awaie* or *my Father did something smack, something grow too; he had a kinde of taste.* The passage as a whole echoes the old morality plays in which the good and bad angels often advised opposite courses of action, and as such it is literary in its affiliations.

If we consider some of these aspects in greater detail, we may note that there is a marked absence of cant, slang and dialect in all Shakespearian plays. No individual is characterised as a cant or slang speaker, though a few words from this register are found. Thus in *The First Part of King Henry the Fourth* Poins uses some example of thieves' cant. He says 'set a match' [Folio *Watch*] for 'plan a robbery' (I ii 104) and 'setter' for 'informant' (II ii 49), but he is not a character who is otherwise noted for his use of this register. The same goes for the other lower-class people in the play. In the same play Prince Hal refers to the language of the 'good Laddes in East-cheape' (II iv 14) but there are no examples of this type of language in the play itself. It is sometimes claimed that Falstaff's *Yedward* for 'Edward' (I ii 130) is a dialect form. This may be so (at least in origin), but it does not suggest that Falstaff was using dialect as a marker of his status. It is the only word he uses which could be claimed as dialect, and it probably has more the status of an affectionate variant than a dialect word. Likewise to say that the omission in the Quarto of the determiner *the* in the Carrier's 'poore Iade is' (II i 6) 'implies rusticity'[3] is to read too much into one form. As we shall see, the use of determiners was much more variable in Elizabethan times than our own, and it is wrong to seize on a particular example as a sign of low-class speech. In this play, then, we find only the occasional use of what might be interpreted as a non-standard feature of language. The examples are so few that they cannot be interpreted as marked features, for the occasional dialect word can as easily be found in verse. Although the play deals ostensibly with low life, what is significant is the absence of low-life language. It is significant because the odd reference to such language in the plays indicates that it was not omitted through ignorance; the choice was deliberate.

Although there are few slang and cant words in the plays, there is a little more dialect. The most important example of dialect is that used by Edgar when his father Gloucester has just thrown himself over the cliffs of Dover – or so he thinks. At first it may seem that Edgar uses the dialect here because he has to adopt the role of a second peasant. In fact he does not use the dialect when speaking to his father, he uses it to disguise himself from Oswald the steward and thus confirms Oswald's opinion of him as a 'bold pezant'. The exchange goes as follows:

> EDG.: Chill not let go Zir, without further 'casion.
> STEW.: Let go Slaue, or thou dy'st.
> EDG.: Good Gentleman goe youre gate, and let poore volke passe: and 'chud ha' bin zwaggerd out of my life, 'twould not ha' bin zo long as 'tis, by a vortnight. Nay, come not neere th'old man: keepe out che vor'ye, or ice try whither your Costward, or my Ballow be the harder; chill be plaine with you.
> STEW.: Out Dunghill.
> EDG.: Chill picke your teeth Zir: come, no matter vor your foynes. (*Lear* IV vi 237–47)

This dialect speech is distinguished from the standard through differences in sound rather than in vocabulary, and these sound differences are principally those of the consonants. Consonants are more stable in English than vowels and so variation among them is more marked. The initial voiceless consonants *s* and *f* are voiced to *z* and *v*. Words like *I*, *will* and *should* are spelt to indicate a variant pronunciation as in *che* 'I' and *chill* 'I will'. One word *casion* 'occasion' appears in a clipped form, though that may not be intended as a dialectal feature. Only the phrase *che vor'ye* may be regarded as a dialectal idiom rather than a variant pronunciation, though it had become a standard feature of this stage dialect. These features were typical of the southern dialects of the Elizabethan period. There are no vocabulary features which indicate the same dialect area. *Costard* occurs in several other Shakespearian contexts; and *ballow* is today a North Midland word and may also have been then. Neither is likely to have been used to represent a peasant dialect speaker. Indeed in this passage Edgar uses more courtly words such as *foynes* 'thrusts with a rapier'. Sounds, and not vocabulary, formed the basis of the peasant dialect.

Edgar's language here is, as already mentioned, the rustic stage dialect of the Elizabethan period. It was used first in the morality plays and then it found its way into such plays as *Ralph Roister Doister*. It may have arisen because the London dialect had originally been a south-eastern one, though in the course of the fifteenth century it changed into a more Midlands variety. When that happened, it is likely that the lower classes in London continued to speak the south-eastern variety so that there were two principal language types in the capital. As the south-eastern variety was spoken by lower-class people in London and by country people to the south of the capital, it became associated with rustic speech. Gradually it became regarded as boorish and provincial, and it was picked up by the dramatists to be used as the stage rustic dialect. It was employed by many of Shakespeare's contemporaries. However, it is important to note that it was used so little by Shakespeare, who evidently felt it to be too blunt an instrument for his type of humour.

Although there may have been two principal language varieties in London at this time, immigration into the capital probably meant that its dialect was then as now the least homogeneous in the country. There was no standardising agency at the time, for the printing press was still not influential enough to affect pronunciation. Many different sounds could be heard in London, and although this may have made the speakers conscious of different accents it also made it difficult to exploit those differences in writing. The stage rustic dialect was useful because it had a recognised place in stage language, and one or two markers like the voicing of initial *s* and *f* were sufficient to identify it. Other dialects would not be so easy to represent because they were not well known on the stage. It is hardly surprising that Shakespeare made little use of dialects in his work and that those dialects he did use were those furthest from the capital (Welsh, Irish and Scots) because they might appear the most distinctive. These dialects are confined to *King Henry the Fifth* and *The Merry Wives of Windsor.* He had plenty of opportunity to exploit differences in speech in his plays, but he chose not to use it. For example, Hotspur calls attention to Owen Glendower's Welsh (*1H4* III i 50) and Orlando comments on the superior accent of the disguised Rosalind who was supposed to come from the country (*AYL* III ii 318).

The dialects are usually represented by one or two key features with accompanying differences from standard English which, though not always of the dialect in question, were intended to suggest the strangeness of the dialect. Thus Welsh is characterised by the use of initial *p* for *b* (*pig* 'big') and *f* for *v* (*falorous* 'valorous') and the repetition of *look you*, and Irish by the representation of *s* and *st* by *sh* (*'tish* ''tis', *Chrish* 'Christ') and the frequent occurrence of *law.* The representation of Scots is difficult because there were no set consonantal changes or well-known idiomatic usages with which to characterise it. Although Captain Jamy's speech does have one or two words like *tway* 'two' and *gud* 'good', whose pronunciation can be considered Scottish, there are many other words whose status is debatable like *theise* 'these' and *de* 'do'. Even today this absence of characteristic markers remains a problem for anyone wanting to represent Scots in literature. Princess Katherine of France is given a mangled form of English which represents a French pronunciation. Among other features she exhibits are the dropping of initial *h* and the corruption of *th to d.*

From these brief examples it can be appreciated that the representation of dialect is a blunt instrument. Provided there are a few unambiguous markers, a dialect can readily be suggested. Yet such a representation must be persevered with and it soon palls; hence Shakespeare used it only for minor characters. Clearly Shakespeare wanted to avoid the easy laugh in preference for the more demanding humour of pun and innuendo. Dialect for him is also not a social concern. The lower-class characters do not use dialect, and Katherine who mangles her English is a princess. Why then did he use it? The answer may be that the 'mistakes' of language are always funny no matter who makes them. Katherine's attempts at English are little different in kind from Dogberry's malapropisms. More importantly the use of dialect in a play like *King Henry the Fifth* underlines the country-wide appeal of the king and reinforces the common theme in Shakespeare that appearances are not the same as reality. A man's accent is no guide to his behaviour, and those who, like Pistol, make assumptions of this sort learn the folly of their own miscalculations.

Contraction, particularly when indicated through apostrophes, is often interpreted as a sign of colloquial speech. It is true that some dialect speakers like Edgar disguised as a peasant or Fluellen are given contracted forms. In Edgar's language quoted above it is likely that *ha'* 'have' was intended to support the dialect features. Unfortunately, it is true not only that many low-class speakers are not given contracted forms, as we saw of Launcelot Gobbo, but also that contractions are found in the language of speakers from all social classes. *Antony and Cleopatra* is a play noted for its rhetorical language, but it also contains many contractions which occur cheek by jowl with the bombast. Cleopatra can address Caesar as 'Sole Sir o' th' World' (V ii 119). The problem with contracted forms, a problem which will be dealt with at greater length in the following chapter, is that they were useful to a dramatist in writing metrical or rhythmical passages. The possibility of using the same word with one syllable more or less was a useful tool in composition. Consequently many contracted forms may not be significant of any speech level. Furthermore, contractions are features of a text which are peculiarly liable to intervention by editors and compositors in their attempts to tidy up the text. It is difficult to be certain that any given text represents Shakespeare's intentions in this matter. At best one might suggest that when contractions are clustered thickly with other features of marked language they may indicate a particular register; otherwise they should not be interpreted as significant.

Swearing and forms of address may also indicate different social status among speakers. The former suffers from some of the same disadvantages as contraction. Many oaths were edited out of the text, particularly after the accession of James I and the campaign against foul language. The Folio differs sharply from some quartos in respect of oaths. Furthermore other oaths may have found their way into the quartos through the enthusiasm of the actors. Oaths and other forms of asseveration do not indicate social standing so much as levels of intimacy among various characters. The more formal the occasion the fewer the oaths. In *The First Part of King Henry the Fourth* Hotspur suggests there is a difference among oaths and he urges his wife to use 'A good mouth-filling Oath: and leaue in sooth' (III i 255), which might imply that the broadest oaths were to be found at the highest and lowest levels of society. Perhaps because there are in the plays so few characters who fill the middle ranks of society, there is little difference to be detected in the oaths used except that the more outrageous characters like Falstaff tend to use the most extravagant oaths. These help to set the seal of humour or intimacy on a scene, though other characters can use them more seriously. In general Shakespeare's oaths avoid the worst excesses found among contemporary plays such as *Gammer Gurton's Needle*, and in this as in so many other linguistic matters he preserves a noteworthy moderation.

Forms of address are naturally adjusted to the social setting in which they occur. As we saw in the Introduction the second person pronoun could be adjusted to the status of the person being addressed. In addition one would address a superior by using the appropriate mode of address such as 'your honour' or 'your worship', whereas equals and inferiors could be addressed less formally. Among more general greetings, it seems that *Good morrow* is relatively neutral, whereas *How now* and *Well met* are characteristically employed to or among lower-class people. Some forms of parting such as Nym's 'Shall wee shogg?' (*H5* II iii 45) are probably slang and are used only to people of the lower classes. The use of personal names is indicative of intimacy, as Falstaff himself indicates when he signs a letter '*Thine, by yea and no: which is as much as to say, as thou vsest him*, Iacke Falstaffe *with my Familiars:* Iohn *with my Brothers and Sister: & Sir* Iohn, *with all Europe*' (*2H4* II ii 124–8). There is, however, considerable variation in the use of names, though the use of Christian names by themselves was less common then than now. The use of both Christian name and surname can be either intimate or slightly condescending. Naturally, the names in the comedies tend towards the humorous, as when Falstaff is addressed as 'Sir Iohn Sacke and Sugar' (*IH4* I ii 109). The names are used for the particular purposes of the drama at any given time, whether that is comedy, opprobrium or whatever, though they can provide a reasonable guide to the level of intimacy and social standing among various characters.

It has been suggested that the so-called ethic dative is indicative of a colloquial style.[4] This dative is particularly associated with the form *me* occurring after verbs where it is superfluous to the sense of the clause. In *Macbeth*, for example, we find 'The clowdy Messenger turnes me his backe' (III vi 41) in which the *me* is irrelevant to the message conveyed by the sentence. The ethic dative was commoner in earlier periods of English and though it is still found in ordinary Elizabethan English, it was probably by then somewhat old-fashioned. As happens so often in language, a form that drops out of the standard language is retained in other varieties, and this happened with the ethic dative. It is for this reason that it can be looked on as an indicator of class, though it is not certain that Shakespeare uses it in this way. It is frequently employed for comedy as in the misunderstanding between Petruchio and Grumio in *The Taming of the Shrew*:

> PETR.: Heere sirra *Grumio*, knocke I say.
> GRU.: Knocke sir? whom should I knocke? Is there any man ha's rebus'd your worship?
> PETR.: Villaine I say, knocke me heere soundly.
> GRU.: Knocke you heere sir? Why sir, what am I sir, that I should knocke you heere sir.
> PETR.: Villaine I say, knocke me at this gate,
> And rap me well, or Ile knocke your knaues pate.
> GRU.: My Mr is growne quarrelsome: I should knocke you first,
> And then I know after who comes by the worst. (I ii 5–14)

In this example it is the master who uses the ethic dative and the servant who misunderstands it. Clearly we have no more than plain comedy here through the exploitation of linguistic variety with no class overtones. Because the ethic dative is treated as comic, it is often found in the speeches of lower-class people, but it should not be interpreted as low. Even when Launce in *Two Gentlemen of Verona* uses it frequently as he does when talking of his dog in IV iv, the intention is to add freshness and vitality to the comedy, not to point to Launce's social origins. Too many examples are spoken by upper-class people for that to be possible; the example quoted from *Macbeth* earlier in the paragraph was spoken by a lord.

A similar explanation probably applies to the not unrelated use of *your* in an indefinite sense. This form is also found in the speeches of low people, though the effect again is probably meant to be humorous rather than socially significant. It is used by Pompey in *Measure for Measure* (IV ii 33), but it is equally used by Iago in *Othello* (II iii 76–7) and especially by Hamlet in 'Your worm is your onely Emperor for diet. . . . Your fat King, and your leane Begger is but variable seruice to dishes.' (IV iii 22–4). All these examples have a touch of humour, even if in the last one the humour is not without its grim side.

Other linguistic features which may indicate different registers are the use of the *do* form of verbs and the variation between *does* and *has* on the one hand and *doth* and *hath* on the other. The *do* form of verbs, as in *he does sing*, is not found in Old English or in other languages cognate with English. We need not concern ourselves with the origin of this form which is the subject of dispute, for all we need to remember is that this form was growing in popularity in the sixteenth century. It was used for emphasis, and there is evidence to suggest that in the Elizabethan period it was also used as part of the elevated style. It is probably not fortuitous in *Hamlet* that many *do* forms occur in the speeches of the players in the play within a play, for their language is notably stilted and hyperbolic. Thus we find, for example:

> I do beleeue you. Think what now you speak:
> But what we do determine, oft we breake. (III ii 181–2)

Even so it should be noticed that not all verbs in this passage or in the speeches as a whole appear in the *do* form, for we must remember that the variants with and without *do* were useful to Shakespeare and other dramatists when they wrote poetry since they could thereby use the same verb with one syllable more or less. As so often with Shakespeare it appears as though the *do* forms may be significant, but are not always so. They may be used to support the high style, and when they occur in association with other features of that style they are probably to be regarded as significant.

The other feature is the variation between *doth* and *does* and between *hath* and *has*. The occurrence of *-(e)th* forms in not only these two but also all other verbs reflects the original southern and midland varieties which formed the basis of the London standard. The northern form in *-(e)s* began to appear in the South in the later Middle Ages and soon grew in popularity. That this northern form is found first in poetry may be an indication that poets were quick to seize the possibility of using variants of the same verb like *cometh/comes* with different syllabic lengths. The *-(e)th* forms continued to be used and they are prominent in the 1611 Bible. In most authors at this time the two forms occur side by side, which could mean that the *-s* form was regarded as new and fashionable and the *-th* form as old-fashioned. It is not in fact easy to decide which of the two was regarded as the more neutral in Shakespeare's day. As far as the variants *hath/has* are concerned the traditional form *hath* was used regularly by Shakespeare throughout his life. On the other hand, *has* is found more frequently in the second half of his career with a sudden surge in usage about the time that plays like *Twelfth Night* and *Hamlet* were written. In these plays *has* occurs frequently in prose and is found particularly in the speech of the comic characters and of lower-class people. The comic characters may be of a high social standing, as is true of Sir Andrew Aguecheek in *Twelfth Night* and Pandarus in *Troilus and Cressida*. Even so not all examples of *has* in these plays occur in the speech of such characters, and there can be little doubt that Shakespeare used *has* in preference to *hath* for purely metrical or syntactic reasons – reasons which have no social or comic implications. In the late plays, although *has* continues to be characteristic of comic and low-class people, it is also used more widely than before by other speakers. The position of the variants *does/doth* is less clear than that of *has/hath*. It seems to echo the general situation of the *has/hath* variants, but the evidence is less straightforward. In other words *has* and *does* may have sociolinguistic overtones indicating a low or comic register, but they can also be used for metrical and syntactic purposes.

It is often said that Shakespeare was very interested in language because he so frequently makes one character comment upon the language of another. In many instances these comments are upon the vocabulary or style used by the other character. It may well be that such comments were necessary because the interpretation of stylistic range was so flexible and had to be pointed to in order to make the correct impact. High-sounding vocabulary may be appropriate in certain people; where it is inappropriate this can be indicated only through the criticism of another character and not through the actual choice of words themselves. Consequently one might state that where deviation in language is not commented on it did not need to be because the audience understood the implications of the deviation quite clearly. Whereas verbal choice is often the butt of criticism, variations in pronunciation are not. Edgar's peasant language receives no comments: it was unambiguous on its own terms. It is important to bear in mind that differences in sound rather than differences in vocabulary were more significant and were so readily understood that they needed no elucidation by the dramatist.

The problem with the different language varieties in Shakespeare is that, although he was evidently familiar with the different registers of his day, he did not go out of his way to use dialect or other marked linguistic items to depict his characters in any consistent or coherent manner. The speech of someone like Fluellen is exceptional. He uses particular linguistic items only occasionally in a significant way, and then it is usually to satisfy the dramatic needs of the moment. They are not employed to help round out a character, and the same item can indeed be used by many diverse characters. The range of significant register is narrower than one might have expected, and it does happen that the dictates of comedy and of social class pull in different directions. Consequently a reader has first to recognise which features may be used to indicate varieties of language and then to isolate those passages in which they are used in a marked way rather than for other non-sociolinguistic reasons. This process is not easy, partly because so little work has been done on Elizabethan English, partly because only the grossest differences of register can be detected in the language of the past, and partly because the text of the plays we read today may not accurately reflect what Shakespeare wrote. Shakespeare's contemporaries noted that he wrote quickly, and the impression of the language of the plays is that he wrote without too much concern for minute linguistic detail except where it could help him develop a particular dramatic point. In this regard syntax is probably more significant than vocabulary. One can be more certain of the significance of the differences of language either when several are grouped together in the same speech or when comment is directed to them, if only obliquely, by another character.

3 Vocabulary

Coleridge's claim that poetry consists of the proper words in their proper order is today accepted as a definition of universal validity. In fact as a definition it raises as many questions as it answers, though it is usually understood to mean that for the poet there is only one word that is suitable for any given place in a poem and that substitution of that word by another leads to a distortion of the poem's meaning. Hence the poet's task is to find the proper word for each slot in his poem. This attitude, however, is not one that can easily be attested before the eighteenth century, and Coleridge's dictum is one that he proclaimed to safeguard an intellectual discovery rather than to describe a situation which had always existed. Certainly for Shakespeare and his contemporaries the substitution of one word for another was a frequent occurrence. The acting environment is one in which changes are naturally proposed. In the extant quartos and folios of the plays there are many differences in vocabulary and some are certainly revisions introduced by Shakespeare or the actors in rehearsal or performance. For example, in *King Lear* the 'Rash boarish fangs' (III vii 57) based on the Quarto appears in the First Folio as 'sticke boarish phangs', a change which Kenneth Muir, the editor of the Arden edition, regards as 'probably an actor's substitution, or a sophistication',[1] for *rash* was a relatively technical word. Many words are altered in the four folios, though such changes were editorial rather than authorial. We today disparage these changes as signs of editorial intervention which does not respect the text's integrity. Respect for the text, however, is a modern convention which few would have understood at that time, and it springs in part from the assumption that poetry represents the proper words in their proper places. It is more likely that Shakespeare himself would have been more in sympathy with his seventeenth-century revisers than with twentieth-century purists, for the former lived nearer his own age and shared some of his assumptions. The ease with which words could be changed may have influenced his attitude towards vocabulary.

Today we divide our vocabulary up into two principal categories, the Anglo-Saxon and the Latin parts, and it is natural to assume that the inkhorn controversy prompted Shakespeare's contemporaries to make a similar division. In *Love's Labour's Lost* Shakespeare seems to reflect this division by letting the pedantic Holofernes use many Latinate words. However, though the inkhorn controversy may have concentrated on borrowings from Greek and Latin because they were the most accessible languages available for such pillaging, the enrichment of the language was by no means confined to classical loans. Even Holofernes can produce an 'extemporal epitaph' on a deer which is written in alliteration, which may well have reminded the audience of the typically English alliterative verse which was by then somewhat provincial:

> The prayfull Princesse pearst and prickt a prettie pleasing Pricket.
> (*LLL* IV ii 53)

When Spenser used archaisms, which were usually of Anglo-Saxon origin, in his poems it was with the intention of ennobling their tone. So it is not without relevance that the following exchange occurs in *Hamlet*:

> 1. PLAY.: But who, O who, had seen the mobled [Folio inobled] Queen.
> HAM.: The mobled Queene?
> POL.: That's good: mobled Queene is good. (II ii 496–8)

Hamlet's reiteration of 'the mobled Queen' is usually taken to imply some questioning on his part of the word *mobled* as though he either found it unsuitable or failed to understand it, though his interjection did not prevent Polonius from applauding the word. Presumably the latter regarded it as a choice epithet, whatever Hamlet's misgivings. Yet *mobled* is not a word of Latin origin. It was probably picked up by Shakespeare from his Warwickshire dialect since it survived there at least till the nineteenth century. There is no earlier instance of its use recorded in the *Oxford English Dictionary*. On another occasion Polonius criticised the word 'beautified' (II ii 110) of Romance origin which he dubbed 'a vilde phrase.' Whatever our views may be about Polonius's taste in such matters, verbal decoration was clearly not just a matter of importing classical words. At all events Shakespeare did not introduce them as slavishly as some of his contemporaries.

The example of *mobled* raises the problem of how many members of an Elizabethan audience would have known the word and how far Shakespeare and other dramatists may have been familiar with the origins of the words they employed. Naturally a learned author like Ben Jonson may have been more acquainted with etymological matters than Shakespeare himself. It is difficult to make any comments on the audience because it embraced a wide range of educational attainment. Furthermore, much that was written then was not necessarily printed so that it would be difficult for many writers or the audience to know what words had been used before. Authors could not easily claim they were the first to use a word in English. There were also no dictionaries at the time. The first produced in England was that compiled by Robert Cawdrey and published in 1604 under the title *A Table Alphabeticall, containing and teaching the true writing and vnderstanding of hard vsual words borrowed from the Hebrew, Greeke, Latine, or French, &c.* This book, as its title implies, seeks to give a definition of the learned words which had been introduced recently into the language, though it also explained some of the archaic words revived by Spenser and his followers. It was not by any means comprehensive even in its modest aims. Evidently there was a need for a work of this kind, which went through several editions, because many were unaware what the high-sounding words that writers were so fond of using meant. If the audience were often puzzled, it is likely that the writers for their part were not always careful about the meanings of the words they used. It would be difficult for a reader or listener to know when the author was using a word with a new sense, whether the meaning he intended was the same as that found in other authors, or whether a classical word was used with the major meaning it had in its parent language. There was no norm or standard against which the audience could measure any interpretation they put upon a particular word. In such a situation the audience would pay more attention to features of language other than meaning. Sound, rhythm, rhetoric and the general drift of a passage would be more important than the precise meaning of individual words. This after all is what many modern audiences do, for their knowledge of Elizabethan English is restricted for different reasons. If audiences reacted like that, then authors may have been less concerned with the precise meaning of their vocabulary and the surface logic of the grammar than with such aspects as sound and rhythm.

Latinate words, being polysyllabic, are often rhythmical and mellifluous and Shakespeare used them for that reason. He did not, however, go out of his way to find strange or exotic words merely to create the impression of learning. He was always quite prepared to accept the interplay of rhythm provided by words of Latin and those of Anglo-Saxon origin. For him there was nothing untoward in such expressions as 'melodious lay [Folio *buy*] To muddy death' (*Ham.* IV vii 183–4), although critics from the eighteenth century like Dr Johnson would regard the use of such words together as a breach of decorum, because *muddy* is more suited to a lower level of poetic expression than the Latinate *melodious*. The use of Latinate words for verbal embellishment did lead to the down-grading of Anglo-Saxon words to some extent. Latinate vocabulary is used for the high style and it would be inappropriate for it to occur in low style scenes. This became more the preserve of Anglo-Saxon words, though contributions from the other modern languages of Europe occur. Anglo-Saxon words, particularly compound words, became stylistically either neutral or low and such compounds are particularly found in insults, because they seem to reflect a more colloquial register, as is true today for such a pair of words as *television* and *goggle-box*. This may be because the joining of two English words together can lead to a massing of consonants and also because Latinate insults are more likely to be witty and learned than earthy. Falstaff can come out with such expressions as 'I am ioyned with no Foot-land-Rakers, no Long-staffe six-penny strikers, none of these mad Mustachio-purple-hu'd-Maltwormes' (*1H4* II i 72–3) when he is talking with lower-class people like Poins. Although *Mustachio* is borrowed from Italian, the other words which go to make up the compounds are of Anglo-Saxon stock. They are felt suitable for this level of language.

An important aspect of the language of the Elizabethan period is the existence of variants. These arose in part through the development of the language and in part through the activity of poets. Such variants may exist at all periods of a language, but in English today they are more restricted and are usually marked. Thus it may be allowable to use either *speciality* or *specialty*, though the latter would to Englishmen be considered an Americanism. The verbs exhibit many variants in the Elizabethan period. The movement of the so-called strong verbs, those that form the preterite by changing the root vowel like *swim – swam*, to weak forms with the preterite formed by adding *-(e)d* resulted in many verbs having both forms. Thus *climbed* and *clomb* were acceptable preterite forms of *to climb*. Within the strong verbs there was a period of adjustment of the different forms because at an earlier period the present, preterite singular, preterite plural and past participle could each have a different vowel. As these forms were gradually reduced to two or at most three different vowels, there was a period when a particular form of a verb could have up to three different manifestations. Thus the preterite of *to write* could be either *writ* or *wrote*, and the past participle might be *writ*, *wrote* or *written*. Although one form may have been commoner than the others, this is not always easy to prove. In any case the use of all forms was quite acceptable and none implied any vulgarity or breach of propriety. In the third person singular it was possible to use the ending *-eth* or *-es*. To take another part of speech, adverbs could be formed with the ending *-ly* or with no ending at all. The learned type of variation arose principally through the use of Latin or Romance affixes. Nouns could be formed through the use of suffixes in *-ure*, *-ment*, or *-ing*, or indeed through the omission of any suffix at all. Verbs could be formed with or without the suffix *-ate*. It was also possible to add the prefix *en-* to existing words to achieve a slightly more elevated form; hence *to paint* could be turned into *to enpaint*.

The use of such variants was a recognised literary technique of the time as Puttenham reveals in his *The Arte of English Poesie*. His chapter on 'auricular figures' opens:

> A word as he lieth in course of language is many wayes figured and thereby not a little altered in sound, which consequently alters the tune and harmonie of a meeter as to the eare. And this alteration is sometimes by *adding* sometimes by *rabbating* [i.e. 'omitting'] of a sillable or letter to or from a word either in the beginning, middle or ending ioyning or vnioyning of sillables and letters suppressing or confounding their seuerall soundes, or by misplacing of a letter, or by cleare exchaunge of one letter for another, or by wrong ranging of the accent. (III 11)

He gives as examples of permissible variants *embolden* for *bolden*, *meeterly* for *meetly*, *spoken* for *spoke*; and *twixt* for *betwixt*, *paraunter* for *parauenture*, and *bet* for *better*. He then continues:

> These many wayes may our maker alter his wordes, and sometimes it is done for pleasure to giue a better sound, sometimes vpon necessitie, and to make vp the rime.

Puttenham's words are echoed in many other rhetorical handbooks from this time.

The recommendations of the rhetoricians indicate that the use of variant forms of the same word was a recognised technique used either to give pleasure through sound or to meet the constraints of metre. Just as the Augustans in the eighteenth century used adjectives in *-y* instead of monosyllabic words to avoid the clash of stresses which would otherwise result, so the Elizabethans used a variety of different forms to achieve the same effect. Clearly the use of variants like *bolden* and *embolden* or *prentice* and *apprentice* allowed a poet to achieve the required balance between stressed and unstressed syllables in his line. This was a useful tool in the composition of blank verse where rhythm was the only feature which revealed that verse was the medium employed. Though the principle is a rhetorical one, it should not be assumed that the resulting words were considered particularly poetic; some, as we have already seen, arose through the ordinary processes of change in the language. The system had many advantages. It provided variety without the necessity of finding different words. It prevented one stress from following another and allowed for the elimination of unnecessary unstressed syllables. This latter aspect meant that utterances did not become too overloaded with weak syllables which could have made them too prosaic or colloquial. It also promoted the coincidence of metrical and verbal stress.[2]

What strikes us today about all this is the emphasis on sound, which is something to which we pay little attention as so many of us read Elizabethan poetry, including that of Shakespeare's plays, silently to ourselves. From earlier poetry most of us are aware of little more variation than the *-ed* form of the preterite and the past participle which can be made to sound as a separate syllable (in which case many editors put an accent over the *e*). This, however, we frequently regard as fussy and so discount it. Few of us know much about Shakespeare's pronunciation and are thus ignorant of the stress patterns of his day. We also frequently read texts in a modern punctuation, the aim of which is to bring out the sense of the passage rather than its rhythm as was more true of Elizabethan punctuation. The result is that we may regard Shakespeare's meaning as more important than the sound of his verse, and we are somewhat nonplussed when we come across passages that seem to have little surface meaning. We are in danger of judging Shakespeare's poetry on premisses different from those on which it was written, and so we may ignore the reasons which led him to choose a particular word.

Sections on figures of sound can be found in all rhetorical handbooks from this period, though they may appear under the guise of schemes of words or of grammar. These figures rely on the repetition of sounds or words in pleasing or significant patterns. Of these we are now familiar only with alliteration though its reputation is much diminished because we tend to think of it as little more than superfluous verbal decoration. Although Shakespeare himself could poke fun at alliteration, as we have seen in the example from *Love's Labour's Lost*, he used it extensively in all his writings in a more serious vein as well. It is, for example, a frequent device in the *Sonnets* where it links together key words and themes, as when he writes:

> The world will waile thee like a makelesse wife,
> The world wilbe thy widdow and still weepe, (9/4–5)

in which the alliteration on *w* is very prominent. However, Elizabethan rhetoric knew many other kinds of repetition beside alliteration, which is often in fact linked with the repetition of words:

> Loue is not loue
> Which alters when it alteration findes,
> Or bends with the remouer to remoue. (116/2–4)

Here the key words in each line are variant forms of the same root and they naturally alliterate together. Often the repetition was less obvious than this and some of the examples we noted in the introduction may easily be overlooked by a modern reader who is not used to noting this type of figure. However, almost all types recommended in the handbooks were used by Shakespeare, for he like other authors found them useful to emphasise parallelism and point the rhythm.

Rhetorical figures are pervasive in the writing of the period and Shakespeare is no exception. Often the rhetoric is close to wit, but almost always it is a type of verbal exhibitionism. In many respects rhetoric was a form of verbal organisation more important than grammar, for no writer would forego a rhetorical figure because it offended grammatical propriety. Indeed, as we have noted, grammar was not yet standardised for English and so its tenets would have had a weak hold over writers. To fill this vacuum left by grammar they employed rhetoric. When Westmoreland says 'This is his Vncles teaching. This is Worcester' (*1H4* I i 96), his words are chosen because of the parallelism emphasised through the anaphora of *this is*. It is unimportant that grammatically the *Worcester* does not echo the possessive *uncle's*. The *Worcester* enables the line to have a strong conclusion and yet to fall into two balanced parts. Similarly in *King Lear* Edmund can say 'An admirable euasion of Whore-master-man, to lay his Goatish disposition on the charge of a Starre' (I ii 121–2). The sentence is divided into two parts, a balance achieved through the omission of the verb. Such a sentence is not colloquial, but rhetorical. Naturally this habit of rhetorical arrangement of clauses and of playing with words, which so often involves ellipsis and non-grammatical constructions, can lead to ambiguity. In particular the process of shortening or lengthening words can readily result in a shortened word, for example, being confused with some other one. In *King John* Pembroke says to the king 'If what in rest you haue, in right you hold' (IV ii 55). Here *rest* can be understood as 'peace' so that the sentence means 'If you rightly possess what you own in peace'. The reference would then be to the kingdom. However, *rest* could be interpreted, and is so understood by some commentators, to be a shortened form of *arrest*, a variant which is met with commonly in Shakespeare. If so, the sentence would mean 'If you are rightly master of him you have arrested' and the reference would then be to Prince Arthur who was imprisoned by John and who was considered to have a better claim to the throne as he was the son of John's older brother. One may assume that such ambiguities were not considered too significant by Shakespeare or his audience. Verbal repetition as recommended by the handbooks could be used by Shakespeare in a fairly mechanical way or in a highly charged utterance as when Lear exclaims: 'Thou'lt come no more, Neuer, neuer, neuer, neuer, neuer.' (*Lear* V iii 307–8). The force of such examples should not mislead us into thinking that Shakespeare exploited rhetorical conventions only for the loftiest thought; they are the backbone of his writing.

The recognition that sound may have dictated the choice among various forms of the same word suggests that the same principle may have been important in choosing between different words of much the same meaning. In many cases Shakespeare may have chosen one word rather than another at any given point in his writing because it had the right number of syllables or because it fitted in with his rhetorical scheme. Many words were borrowed from Latin at this time precisely because they sounded better and not because they signified something that had not till then been expressed in English. Words like *see* and *perceive* were probably distinguished only at a stylistic level and not at a semantic one. It is only because the two words have existed for some time in the language that a certain specialisation of meaning has since taken place. Consequently we should hesitate to interpret the meanings of Shakespeare's words too rigorously because they may have been chosen for quite different reasons: the stylistic level appropriate to the context and the effect of the sound pattern. Equally he may have been less worried than we are by word-substitutions made by actors and editors provided the sound-pattern and rhythm were maintained. Naturally it is difficult to prove or disprove this view since we know so little about how Shakespeare constructed his lines or how much he altered them to achieve the desired effect. Nevertheless the evidence certainly points in that direction. The same may equally apply to some of the less usual words he employs, some of which have been discovered by Hilda Hulme in local records.[3] The word *cradle-clothes* (*1H4* I i 88) is found also in a Stratford inventory and it may be a local word. Shakespeare would not expect his audience to react to it in a special way and recognise its origins. Words were less powerfully localised and less semantically strong then; they were more in the nature of stylistic counters.

That Shakespeare thought along these lines is also suggested by the way he handles his sources. As long ago as the eighteenth century Richard Farmer claimed that 'our Authur hath done little more than throw the very words of North into blank verse.'[4] Anyone who has compared a play like *Antony and Cleopatra* with North's version will recognise what Farmer meant, even if he expresses it more directly than we might care for today. We do not emphasise this aspect of Shakespeare's composition because we feel it undervalues his work as a poet if he merely took over what was in front of him instead of searching long and hard for the right word. Consider for example the famous description of Cleopatra on her barge:

> The Barge she sat in, like a burnisht Throne
> Burnt on the water: the Poope was beaten Gold,
> Purple the Sailes: and so perfumed that
> The Windes were Loue-sicke.
> With them the Owers were Siluer,
> Which to the tune of Flutes kept stroke, and made
> The water which they beate, to follow faster;
> As amorous of their strokes. For her owne person,
> It beggerd all discription, she did lye
> In her Pauillion, cloth of Gold, of Tissue,
> O're-picturing that Venus, where we see
> The fancie out-worke Nature. On each side her,
> Stood pretty Dimpled Boyes, like smiling Cupids,
> With diuers coulour'd Fannes whose winde did seeme,
> To gloue the delicate cheekes which they did coole,
> And what they vndid did. (II ii 195–209)

This passage which seems quintessentially Shakespearian is based on the following section of North's *Plutarch.*

> . . . she made so light of it and mocked Antonius so much that she disdained to set forward otherwise but to take her barge in the river of Cydnus, the poop whereof was of gold, the sails of purple, and the oars of silver, which kept stroke in rowing after the sound of the music of flutes, howboys, citherns, viols, and such other instruments as they played upon in the barge. And now for the person of herself: she was laid under a pavilion of cloth of gold of tissue, apparelled and attired like the goddess Venus commonly drawn in picture; and hard by her, on either hand of her, pretty fair boys apparelled as painters do set forth god Cupid, with little fans in their hands, with the which they fanned wind upon her.[5]

The poetry is modelled on the prose and many of the words are taken straight over, even if some of the more telling effects are introduced by Shakespeare. It is not necessary to analyse the passage in detail to see that Shakespeare for the most part appropriated the vocabulary which North offered him and simply rearranged the words into a rhetorical and rhythmical pattern. Choice of vocabulary was less important than its use and deployment, which meant ransacking the resources of rhetoric. He picked up the words immediately available and turned them into powerful poetry; in no sense did he go out of his way to look for significant vocabulary.

As part of Shakespeare's habit of repetition it has been noted that he sometimes seizes on a particular word which he uses frequently in one play. Although words like *honest* in *Othello* and *honour* in *The First Part of King Henry the Fourth* are part of the everyday language, they had particular connotations in the Elizabethan period. Another such word is *nothing*, a word which may readily be overlooked by a modern reader. Because it represents 0 it can be used bawdily, as in *Hamlet*:

HAM.: That's a faire thought to ly between Maids legs
OPHE.: What is my lord?
HAM.: Nothing. (III ii 114–16)

It does, nevertheless, have a much profounder sense, which may indeed have added spice to the bawdy innuendoes. For in theological terms creation was constructed out of nothing, and this view held by Christians was in opposition to the view of creation held by pagans. Furthermore, all created things consist essentially of nothing, which is why man is so foolish to hanker after material things. This concept was assisted by the echo of *thing* and *nothing*. It may therefore have seemed almost blasphemous to the audience when Lear says 'Nothing can be made out of nothing ' (*Lear* I iv 132), because in Christian belief so much had indeed been made by God out of nothing. By the same token it may be that the title *Much Ado About Nothing* is rather more pointed than modern audiences think. Because we today think of the Elizabethan period as an age of bombast we tend to think that only the heavy words are significant. In fact, many of the more ordinary words were charged with meaning through the controversies of the time, and it is important to pay attention to them.[6]

It may be that many words had a contemporary significance which is difficult now for us to understand because they helped to make up the Elizabethan way of thinking. Other words can be made to appear to have an extra significance when they form part of some witty exchange, though that significance is put on them by Shakespeare himself. Thus when Touchstone says 'I am heere with thee, and thy

Goats, as the most capricious Poet honest *Ouid* was among the Gothes' (*AYL* III iii 4–6), he uses *capricious* not so much in its more usual meaning of 'unpredictable, fantastic', but in its etymological meaning, for the word is derived from the Latin *capra* 'a female-goat'. Such hidden meanings should be explained in a competent edition and need not detain us. Less often explained are the more poetic types of word, particularly examples of functional shift, the name given to the process whereby a word which normally fulfils one function, such as a noun, in English is used in a different function, such as a verb. The meaning of such words may not always be clear simply because it is not evident in some instances what function a given word may have – a difficulty which can be exacerbated by the variety in word order found in Elizabethan English. Thus in *Timon of Athens* we find a sentence apparently consisting of three nouns 'Destruction phang mankinde' (IV iii 23). The Folio reading has the added difficulty of the spelling *phang* for 'fang'. It is normal to think that one of these nouns has been shifted to a verb, and our modern word order encourages us to assume that *phang* is here a verb expressing the optative with the metaphorical meaning 'may destroy'. This presumably is the correct interpretation. It should, however, be mentioned that *destruction* is used as a verb by Shakespeare and so the sentence could be understood to involve the inverted word order of verb and subject, which could then have the sense 'May fangs destroy mankind'. Although this latter interpretation seems less likely, there is nothing in Shakespeare's language which prevents it and it may not in other instances be so easy to tell what is the correct interpretation.

Functional shift occurred in Shakespeare because of its frequency in the language of his time. It is a feature of language which becomes possible as the inflectional endings of words, which indicate their grammatical relationships, decay so that there is no apparent difference between one part of speech and another. Thus today the word *round* can be a verb, noun, preposition, adjective or adverb; its function is revealed only through the context. English had begun life as an inflected language, but the inflections had gradually fallen during the Middle English (*c.*1100–1500) period so that by the Elizabethan age there was often no morphological distinction between various parts of speech. The Elizabethans made use of this new freedom by employing words for many different functions. Theoretically that freedom is still available today, but the presence of dictionaries acts as a brake upon it because many people think they dictate what class particular words fall into. Furthermore, the inheritance of the eighteenth-century grammarians has been the restriction of the scope of this particular activity. Hence Shakespeare lived after the time when functional shift became possible in the history of English but before the time when advances in scholarship and education restricted the use of that freedom. Shakespeare, as so often, both used this freedom and made fun of it. In *The Merry Wives of Windsor* he is able to expose the excesses of functional shift by giving Evans some examples of it not found elsewhere in his writings. He says 'I will description the matter to you' (I i 196) and 'But can you affection the 'o-man' (I i 207) with *description* and *affection* used as verbs. These new verbs are more concrete than 'describe' and 'affect', though they have not been adopted in the language. Nevertheless this parody here did not prevent Shakespeare from using the form extensively.

Some examples of functional shift from *Antony and Cleopatra* will exhibit its range and some of its difficulties. Act III opens with Ventidius saying 'Now darting Parthya art thou stroke'. The modifier *darting* is here based on a verb 'to dart', which is a functional shift of the noun *dart* 'an arrow'. The Parthians were renowned for their habit of shooting arrows from horseback, particularly as they withdrew from a charge. This use of *darting* is echoed in *stroke*, since the nation which usually fires arrow has now been hit itself. But the reader or listener might easily understand *darting* to mean 'moving quickly backwards and forwards', since that is the usual meaning of the verb. No earlier examples of this modifier are found in the *Oxford English Dictionary* before Shakespeare, though the verb *dart* 'to cast javelins or shoot arrows' is found earlier. The example reveals that the extension of meaning of words already in the language could lead to potential confusion between homonyms. In the previous scene Caesar commenting on the excesses of the feast remarks 'the wilde disguise hath almost Antickt vs all' (II vii 122–3). Here Shakespeare has used the noun *antic(k)* 'a grotesque play, or someone who performs in such a play' into a verb presumably meaning 'to make a buffoon of'. In this sense Shakespeare's example is the first recorded in the *Oxford English Dictionary*. The problem is to know which of the senses of the noun may be invoked in the verbal form and whether the latter carries with it some of the connotations of disapproval associated with the former. Because the word is newly minted, it seems to carry less disapproval and criticism. Earlier in the play Cleopatra criticised Charmian and said:

> By *Isis*, I will giue thee bloody teeth,
> If thou with *Cæsar* Paragon againe:
> My man of men. (I v 70–2)

Here *paragon* means 'compare, contrast' and in this meaning is found in other Elizabethan writers. Shakespeare, however, uses the word in two different meanings, both of which are closer to the meaning of the noun. In *Othello* Cassio says 'he hath atchieu'd a Maid That paragons description' (II i 61–2), where the meaning is 'excels', as a paragon ought. In *King Henry the Eighth* the king says of his wife 'the primest Creature That's Parragon'd o'th'World' (II iv 229–30), where the sense is 'proclaimed as a model'. In these two senses the Shakespearian usages are unique. One word can be extended in many ways, but such extensions can pose problems for the reader which are accentuated by the word's apparent familiarity.

It is no accident that the three words quoted as examples of functional shift in the last paragraph are all cases of the use of nouns as verbs, for this is the most common variety of functional shift. It is the nouns which are the most concrete parts of speech and their use as verbs helps to make the language even more compressed with meaning. They add immediacy and they provide a striking quality to the language. They enable the sense to be expressed elliptically and evocatively at one and the same time. It is this variety of functional shift which helps to make Shakespeare's language so vivid.

However, functional shift is only one aspect of Shakespeare's extension of the vocabulary. He frequently takes a word and extends its meaning without altering the function. Often this may be accomplished through a metaphorical meaning, but it may also be done through other processes. Punning is a frequent source of verbal enlargement. This is achieved partly through the use of new meanings and partly through the use of prefixes and suffixes to create a different word. When in *The First Part of King Henry the Fourth* Falstaff finds that his horse has been removed he exclaims 'What a plague meane ye to colt me thus?' where *colt* has the meaning 'trick'. To this Henry replies 'Thou ly'st, thou art not colted, thou art vncolted' (II ii 36–7). Here Shakespeare has invented a new word *vncolted* simply for the services of the pun, and it exhibits how ready he was to play with words. On other occasions he can take a common word and use it in a new sense. Cleopatra says of her revels with Antony 'Ere the ninth houre, I drunke him to his bed' (*Ant* II v 21), where *drunke* means 'made him so drunk that he had to take to his bed' and this sense is not recorded elsewhere. A more metaphoric extension of a word occurs when Agricola says of Antony's use of Cleopatra 'He ploughd her, and she cropt' (*Ant* II ii 232). The image is from agriculture, though the verb *crop* is not usually intransitive. It here has the sense 'produced fruit, i.e. gave birth to the child Caesarion'. It is readily comprehensible from the normal meaning of the verb, but it stretches it in an unusual direction.

One final type of verbal ingenuity may be mentioned, for it has connections with punning and the wider question of verbal enlargement. It is the ability to unite a passage by using words which overlap in their semantic fields, even though the primary meaning intended in the passage is not that which creates an echo with other words. It is a technique which has attracted attention for a long time; it was apparently first noted by W. Whiter in his *A Specimen of a Commentary on Shakespeare* from 1794. A passage that Whiter noted was from *Coriolanus*:

besides, forget not
With what Contempt he wore the humble Weed,
How in his Suit he scorn'd you: but your Loues,
Thinking vpon his Seruices, tooke from you
Th'apprehension of his present portance,
Which most gibingly, vngrauely, he did fashion
After the inueterate Hate he beares you. (II iii 217–23)

Whiter picked out from this speech the words *weed – suit – seruices – fashion*. The first word *weed* refers to clothes, with the sense of *the humble weed* being a metaphorical expression implying a suit of humility. In the next line *suit* refers to the petitionary address by Coriolanus but it readily in another sense picks up the idea of 'dress' from *weed*. Then *seruices* can be linked to *suit*, partly because those who perform services may naturally expect their suits to be favourably received, but also because *suit* can have an additional meaning of 'livery' which is worn by those who perform services. The final word *fashion* is naturally linked with clothes, though it is here used as a verb rather than a noun. Other words might be linked with this scheme, for *portance* implies the grand style with which one bears oneself, a word which relates easily to fashion. This type of submerged linking is found frequently in Shakespeare[7] and provides some of the poetry's sinewy strength.

Shakespeare is thus very much of his time in seeking to extend the vocabulary of the language of his time. He simply does it in an unconventional way. He does not look for the hard or Latinate word, and therefore his language has less of that surface difficulty found in Ben Jonson. It is much easier to think one understands Shakespeare because his linguistic innovations are concentrated in the more everyday words. He extends their meanings through functional shift or through metaphor or through emphasising some less frequent element in its make-up. In this way he was able to write poetry which was densely packed with meaning but which did not seem strange or exotic.

4 The Nominal Group

The nominal group may be defined briefly as a group of words which can act as the subject of a sentence.[1] As we noted in the Introduction it is usual to posit that the nominal group in Modern English contains four elements: determiner, modifier, head and qualifier. The head is that part of the group upon which all the other elements depend and is the only obligatory element. The modifier and qualifier are those elements which precede and follow the head respectively and are defined formally by their position in relation to the head. There is theoretically no limit to the number of modifiers and qualifiers each head can carry. The determiner in Modern English precedes the modifier and consists of a small group of words like the articles and possessive and demonstrative pronouns which are mutually exclusive; there can be only one determiner per head in each nominal group. One cannot say in Modern English *the his book*. Hence the nominal group 'The beautiful, young girl with the black hair sitting in the corner' consists of the determiner *the*, two modifiers *beautiful* and *young*, the head *girl*, and two qualifiers *with the black hair* and *sitting in the corner*. It is characteristic of Modern English that whereas modifiers consist usually of single words like *beautiful*, though they can be modified by an intensifier like *very*, qualifiers are usually phrases such as *with the black hair*. This particular qualifier consists in its turn of a preposition and a subordinate nominal group (determiner, modifier, head). Of the two major sentence groups in English, the nominal and the verbal, it is the former which can be expanded at will and which carries the weight of descriptive meaning in a sentence. This is as true of Elizabethan English as it is today. Compared with prose, poetry of all ages exhibits looser organisation in the structure of the nominal group, particularly in the matter of qualifiers. In modern prose it would be normal to have qualifiers which are quite tightly structured so that the sense is clear, whereas in poetry the relation of the qualifiers to the head is much looser. This is also the case in Elizabethan poetry. Thus in *Macbeth* we find the famous description of sleep:

> Sleepe that knits vp the rauel'd Sleeue of Care,
> The death of each dayes Life, sore Labors Bath,
> Balme of hurt Mindes, great Natures second Course,
> Chiefe nourisher in Life's Feast. (II ii 37–40)

In this passage each of the qualifiers starting from *The death of each dayes Life* stands only in a loose relationship to the head *Sleepe*, because each qualifier introduces a new metaphor which is itself a nominal group in apposition to the head. Each separate nominal group is related only by sense to the head, and not by any grammatical mechanism. However in a longer passage from *The First Part of King Henry the Fourth*, the qualifiers are more tightly organised:

> A Post from Wales, loaden with heauy Newes;
> Whose worst was, That the Noble *Mortimer*,
> Leading the men of Herefordshire to fight
> Against the irregular and wilde *Glendower*,
> Was by the rude hands of that Welshman taken,
> And a thousand of his people butchered:
> Vpon whose dead corpes there was such misuse,
> Such beastly, shamelesse transformation,
> By those Welshwomen done, as may not be
> (Without much shame) retold or spoken of. (I i 37–46)

In this passage everything depends upon *Post* 'messenger' in a logical way that is made clear through the grammar. The preposition *from* and the participial adjective clearly relate to *Post* grammatically. The other parts within the qualifier are likewise grammatically tied in: thus *whose* depends upon *newes*, and *Leading* upon *Mortimer*; *Vpon whose* refers to *people*, and the final *as may not be retold* expands the *done* immediately before. This is a type of subordinate qualification as compared with the co-ordinate qualification of the *Macbeth* passage. Subordinate qualification is more prosaic, because it is more often used, as here, to put across information. One therefore finds it in historical plays and in opening or closing scenes where the background to or conclusion of the drama is being expounded. Co-ordinate qualifiers are used in more poetic passages. Hence the type of qualifier used in a scene may contribute an important aspect of its tone.

Before considering some of the problems of organisation in the nominal group, it may be appropriate to examine some of the difficulties that arise for a modern reader in trying to analyse a Shakespearian nominal group. These difficulties can arise because the organisation of the nominal group was more flexible then so that it may be almost impossible to decide which part of the nominal group is the head and which the modifier and so on. Today, as we noted, modifiers are single words and qualifiers phrases, but in Elizabethan English qualifiers can be single words and modifiers may, though less commonly, be phrases. Hence in a nominal group like 'Militarie Title Capitall' (*1H4* III ii 110) there is nothing which can formally distinguish the head from the modifiers and/or qualifiers. Any of the three words could act as the head (for each is capitalised in the First Folio) and any could equally act as modifier or qualifier. In fact in this instance *Title* is the head, *Militarie* a modifier, and *Capitall* a qualifier; and the phrase has the sense 'pre-eminent military reputation'. However, modern students, particularly when reading the text, will be tempted to take *Capitall* as the head because this would be the case in Modern English structure. A phrase like 'generall Enemy Ottoman' (*Oth.* I iii 49) might be interpreted in the same way as 'Militarie Title Capitall', though in this case other interpretations are possible and perhaps even more likely. Moreover, the frequency in Elizabethan English of functional shift, whereby one part of speech is used as another, and the daringly imaginative examples of functional shift found in Shakespeare's plays can make it difficult to decide what words actually belong to any given nominal group. In the following passage from *Twelfth Night* the punctuation in the First Folio suggests that *mellow* is a verb:

O that I seru'd that Lady,
And might not be deliuered to the world
Till I had made mine owne occasion mellow
What my estate is. (I ii 41–4)

Nevertheless, many editors put a comma after *mellow* and interpret it as an adjective and so presumably part of a nominal group.[2] In *Antony and Cleopatra* (II ii 236) the problems are partly of functional shift and partly of the wider organisational pattern. The line in the Folio reads 'And breathlesse powre breath forth'. Here *breathlesse* can be understood as a modifier to the head *powre* which could be the object complement of the verb *breath* with the sense 'and breathes out breathless charm' or it can be taken as the qualifier to the *she* found in the previous line and hence as the subject of the verb *breath* with the tense 'And she breathless breathes forth charm'. If *breathlesse* is taken as a qualifier to *she*, as is often done in modern editions, it opens up the possibility of taking *powre* as a verb and *breath* as its object complement (i.e. as a nominal group rather than as a verb), thereby enabling *breath(lesse)* and *breath* to be more closely linked in sound and function in the manner so common in Shakespeare; and then the meaning would be 'And breathless she pours forth breath'. This option is concealed in editions with a modernised spelling in which the editors take *breath* as a verb, for then it will appear in the form *breathe.* If, however, *breath* is taken as a nominal group rather than as a verb, it would mean that *powre* is better understood as the verb 'pour' rather than the functionally shifted verb 'power'. When *powre* is understood as a noun, as is the case for example in the Arden edition of this play,[3] it has to be understood in an otherwise unattested sense of 'charm'. Although the choice among these options will be a subjective editorial one, the point I wish to stress is how difficult it is to decide precisely what constitutes a given nominal group.

A different problem is presented by a nominal group like 'A brothers dead loue' (*TN* I i 31). In this instance the difficulty is created by the number of variables that have to be considered. As we have seen a qualifier can be a single word in Elizabethan English so that one variable concerns *dead* which can be either a qualifier to *brothers* or a modifier to *loue.* Although it might seem less usual to have a qualifier to a possessive like *brothers*, this was an acceptable construction at the time as in 'With them a Bastard of the Kings deceast' i.e. of the dead King's (*John* II i 65). What would perhaps be less common even for Elizabethan English is that *brothers*, which is itself a modifier to *loue*, should have a qualifier. A second variable concerns the type of possessive represented by *brothers.* In Elizabethan English it was possible to have either a subjective or an objective genitive, though only the former is found in modern usage. The difference between these two possessives may be perceived by thinking of the head as a verb and the possessive as either its subject or its object. Shakespeare's *brothers loue* could mean either the love for someone else by the brother or the love for the brother by someone else. The latter interpretation is the objective genitive and its acceptability in Shakespearian English can be appreciated from such examples as 'And do inuite you to my Sisters view' (*Ant.* II ii 171), which means that Antony is invited to see the speaker's, i.e. Caesar's, sister. With these two variables alone, this nominal group's grammar can produce four acceptable interpretations. The decision among them can be made only on subjective grounds from the context in which the nominal group occurs, and naturally some readers may arrive at varying conclusions.

When faced with a nominal group it is important to establish first what is its head, though as should now be clear that may not be easy. The absence of some marks of punctuation in early seventeenth-century English and hence in the First Folio is a complicating factor. The apostrophe representing a plural possessive was not employed by them and so the absence of the sign cannot be interpreted to mean that a possessive was not intended. In *Antony and Cleopatra* there are different interpretations of the following lines:

> Eternity was in our Lippes, and Eyes,
> Blisse in our browes bent . . . . (I iii 35–6)

Modern editors usually punctuate the last nominal group as *brows' bent* and take *bent* to be a substantive meaning 'arch', as in the Alexander and Arden editions. There are other passages in Shakespeare which suggest a link between eyes or looks and a substantive *bent*, though the latter does not in those instances mean 'arch'. One example occurs in *King Henry the Fifth*:

> Your eyes which hitherto haue borne
> In them against the French that met them in their bent . . . .
> (V ii 15–16)

However, it is equally likely that *bent* is a qualifier to the head *browes* for bent in the sense 'arched' collocates frequently at this time with *brows* (*cf. OED Bent, ppl.a.* lb) though parallels are lacking in Shakespeare. Furthermore, that the first line in the quotation from *Antony and Cleopatra* has *Lippes, and Eyes* as a head suggests that in the second *browes* would be a more suitable head than *bent.* The meaning is not much affected whichever reading is adopted, though the rhythm and stress could be.

The question of what forms the head of a nominal group may also be considered in relation to the following examples. In *Antony and Cleopatra* Antony says as he leaves Cleopatra to return to Rome:

> I go from hence
> Thy Souldier, Seruant, making Peace or Warre,
> As thou affects. (I iii 69–71)

The punctuation in modern editions, following that of the First Folio, indicates that there are two nominal groups with *Souldier* and *Seruant* as their respective heads. That is, Antony is going both as Cleopatra's soldier and as her servant – two attributes which are linked only by their contiguity in the line. However, the qualifier which follows *Seruant* suggests that Antony will serve Cleopatra in the wars he makes and that consequently there is a much closer connection between the two words *Souldier* and *Seruant*. This could be achieved by repunctuating the half-line as *Thy Souldier Seruant* or even as *Thy Souldier-Seruant*. The absence of a comma after *Souldier* would also allow the two halves of the line to balance each other rhythmically. After all a few lines later Cleopatra wishes Antony:

> Vpon your Sword
> Sit Lawrell victory, and smooth successe
> Be strew'd before your feete. (I iii 99–101)

Here editors do not put a comma after *Lawrell*, which they presumably understand as a modifier to *victory* or as a quasi-compound as though Shakespeare meant *Lawrell-victory*. (To take *victory* as a qualifier to *Lawrell* as though the phrase meant 'victory laurel' would be possible in Elizabethan English, but this structure is hardly likely to have much appeal for modern readers, though the sense is excellent.) In this line it is partly the absence of a comma in the First Folio and the balance of the second nominal group *smooth successe* which have prevented editors from understanding *Lawrell* and *victory* as two separate heads. It may also be significant that *Lawrell* and *victory* have an identical meaning, whereas *Souldier* and *Seruant* are contrastive. Nevertheless, the yoking together of opposites is a common feature of Elizabethan conceits.

These two examples have apparently similar structures, but they are interpreted differently. In the case of *Lawrell victory*, it is not usual for modern editors to add a hyphen, for they tend not to do so with the heads of nominal groups if there is no lead in the Folio text. A hyphen may be introduced by editors if there is none in the Folio when the two words form a modifier rather than a head, as in 'I am marble-constant' (*Ant.* V ii 238); here the Folio reads *Marble constant.* Why it should be necessary to hyphenate here rather than elsewhere is not clear, but the propriety of hyphenation will be considered presently since it does involve modifiers as well as heads. It is noteworthy, though, that a hyphen is introduced by editors in another line in *Antony and Cleopatra*, though there is none in the Folio, which reads:

> But let the world ranke me in Register
> A Master leauer, and a fugitiue. (IV ix 21–2)

Modern editors read *master-leauer* as a compound, though one might suggest that the hyphen is unhappy, because the Folio's *Master* may refer both to *leauer* and to *fugitiue*; at least that would give the line its most pointed reading.

Examples like *Souldier, Seruant* and *Lawrell victory*, however punctuated, show that Shakespeare frequently put two substantives together either as a witty contrast or as a metaphorical extension to each other. It is perhaps surprising that this recognition does not prevent editors from emending some lines where such groups occur. An interesting example occurs in *Antony and Cleopatra* in the lines which read in the Folio:

> but all the charmes of Loue,
> Salt *Cleopatra* soften thy wand lip,
> Let Witchcraft ioyne with Beauty, Lust with both. (II i 20–2)

Modern editors prefer to read *wan'd* for *wand*, which is then often explained as meaning 'declined, gone off from its perfection like the moon which wanes'. Others interpret *wan'd* as a variant spelling for *wanned* 'darkened, blackened'. No one keeps *wand*, which could refer to a magic wand as used by sorcerers. As we saw in the last chapter, it is customary for Shakespeare to carry some idea or metaphor through several lines, and in this passage it might be suggested that *charmes – wand – Witchcraft* decorate a single idea through the choice of related words. It is also quite possible to have two substantives thrown together where one extends the metaphorical significance of the other; in this case Cleopatra might well have lips that charm, for in the next line witchcraft is said to team up with beauty. On the other hand, there is no indication in this scene that Cleopatra is old or ugly, which *wan'd* and *wanned* imply. The emphasis is entirely on her almost supernatural powers and sensuality. The question may well be whether *wand lip* is too daring and inventive a phrase for us to accept even from Shakespeare. It is probably little more than habit which allows us to accept some new startling expressions from him, but not others: we readily accept only those hallowed by the editorial tradition.

Editors may naturally rearrange the punctuation of the Folio to arrive at a different head from the one found there. Thus the Folio's 'all-honor'd, honest, Romaine Brutus' (*Ant.* II vi 16) often appears in modern editions, as in the Arden Shakespeare, as *all-honour'd, honest Roman, Brutus* whereby the head of the nominal group becomes *Roman*, and *Brutus* is relegated to the role of qualifier. Both structures are quite acceptable in Elizabethan, as in Modern, English, and it is not clear why some modern editors wish to break away from the Folio here since its reading might be thought preferable rhythmically. It is of course true that the use of adjectives as heads of nominal groups is a regular feature of Shakespearian English, although it has ceased to be generally possible in modern structure. The occurrence of adjectives in this position may cause some difficulty for the reader in that adjectives indicate a quality and it is often possible to relate that quality to an individual or to a wider human type. Perhaps the two are not far apart. Certainly the link of the adjective head with abstracts to express the actions of humans gives the language at once a particular and a general reference which is lacking in Modern English. Thus when Achilles says:

> 'Tis certaine, greatnesse once falne out with fortune,
> Must fall out with men too: what the declin'd is,
> He shall as soone reade in the eyes of others (*Troil.* III iii 75–7)

the reference of *the declin'd* is to a type expressed through an individual, in this case Achilles himself. In this it is accentuated by the use of *greatnesse*. A similar example is:

> How easie is it, for the proper false
> In womens waxen hearts to set their formes (*TN* II ii 28–9)

except that *proper false* here takes the plural form *their* instead of the singular. In another passage the abstract honour can be either personal or general:

> What shall you aske of me that Ile deny,
> That honour (sau'd) may vpon asking giue. (*TN* III iv 201–2)

Whether one takes *honour* as the subject of the *may giue* or as part of an absolute participial construction, it is possible to interpret it as referring specifically to the honour of the speaker, in this case Olivia, or to the honour of all women who might be asked for something by their beloved. This ability to write at the personal and the general level at one and the same time is an important strength in Shakespeare's writings which helps to give them that timeless and universal appeal. It is, however, achieved through exploiting a particular structure in the language at the time.

An interesting aspect of *the proper false* quoted above is that the nominal group consists of two adjectives and that consequently it is not possible to tell which is the head. Because a qualifier can be a single word in Elizabethan times, the expression may mean 'the handsome if they are false' or 'the false if they are handsome', though modern readers are likely to prefer the latter because of the restrictions in present-day structure. It is also possible to assume that *proper false* is a single head and should be hyphenated rather in the manner that was suggested for *Souldier-Seruant* earlier in this chapter, though this alternative is not adopted in modern editions. Nevertheless, when two adjectives do occur together whether in the modifier position or not they may be hyphenated by modern editors as in 'More active-valiant or more valiant-young' (*1H4* V i 90), where the Folio reads 'More actiue, valiant, or more valiant yong'. The result is that it is not untypical to find a modern edition of Shakespeare having the following types of punctuation:

(i) Two adjectives in a modifer slot which are separated by a space, but no comma, as in 'A very dishonest paltry boy' (*TN* III iv 369) or 'a headstrong potent fault' (*TN* III iv 194). The Folio also has no hyphens here.

(ii) Two adjectives in a modifier slot which are hyphenated, as in 'Of honourable-dangerous consequence' (*JC* I iii 124). There is no hyphen in the Folio.

(iii) Two adjectives in a modifer slot which are separated by a comma, but which are interpreted by the editor as being linked in meaning. In 'I will bee strange, stout, in yellow stockings' (*TN* II v 152) the *strange, stout* is interpreted by the editors of the Arden edition as 'firmly aloof'.[4] The commas are taken over from the Folio.

This diversity is regrettable in modern editions which are supposedly punctuated and spelt in a modern way and which are designed to help a reader today understand Shakespeare more easily. It springs from an unwillingness to depart too far in this particular aspect of punctuation from the Folio text and also perhaps from our own uncertainties about punctuation in modern spelling. The punctuation in a *headstrong potent fault* should suggest to the reader that the fault is overwhelmingly potent rather than that it is both potent and irresistible; but the reader is not certain which is meant. The problem is that modern editors adopt modern spelling and punctuation conventions for the most part. For example, they introduce capitals in line with modern usage. Yet, with commas, fullstops and hyphens their courage deserts them and they often try to arrive at some compromise with the Folio text so that their punctuation is neither modern nor Elizabethan. This compromise suggests that many editors have not decided for themselves precisely what Shakespeare's words mean in certain passages. In this respect recent editors are more bound by the Folio than those in the nineteenth century. Abbott in his *A Shakespearian Grammar* understands 'any moment leisure' (*Ham.* I iii 133) as a grand compound *any-moment-leisure*.[5] Most twentieth-century editors would not introduce hyphens here, though they also do not give the reader any indication how to understand this expression. Is *moment* part of the head or is it a modifier? Elizabethan punctuation is different from modern punctuation, and a student who has never seen a copy of the Folio will not understand why punctuation is present in some passages, but missing in others. Why is it *moment leisure*, but 'minute-while' (*1H6* I iv 54, where the Folio has 'Minute while'), or why is it *headstrong potent*, but *marble-constant* (where the Folio has no hyphen) in modern editions? It may be, of course, that the editors assume that Shakespeare was himself not as concerned with the meaning of his words as with their rhythm in the line; and I think there is much to be said for this view, though it runs counter to many modern critical assumptions. If an editor does feel this, he should nevertheless make this opinion clear to his readers so that they can understand the principles of his punctuation.

Hyphenation and punctuation can of course make great differences in some passages, and the compromise solutions followed by modern editors inevitably leave modern readers floundering. In *The Winter's Tale* Hermione says:

> I loue thee not a Iarre o'th'Clock, behind
> What Lady she her Lord. (I ii 43–4)

Older commentators understood *lady-she* as a compound and took it to be of the same type as *moment-while*. The sense was then 'less than any woman loves her husband'. Some editors omit the hyphen and keep the Folio's capitals and interpret *Lady* as a modifier with the meaning 'aristocratic'. Others omit the hyphens and use lower case letters for *lady* and *lord*. In such cases the editor may understand *lady she* to be a compound, even though the two words are not hyphenated, or he may understand ellipsis with the sense 'less than any lady as she may love her lord'. Other examples like this are common enough.

The interpretation of some nominal groups is complicated by the existence in English of older possessive forms which had no inflectional *-s*. In Modern English *ladychapel* comes from *lady chapel*, i.e. 'chapel of Our Lady', in which *lady* is an old feminine noun without a possessive inflexion. This may have influenced some groups in Elizabethan English. To Shakespeare there may have been little difference between *heart blood* and *heart's blood*, though the former is often compounded. Some groups may have adopted this arrangement, even though the words which are possessive do not descend from Old English inflectional categories without *-s*. Thus in *Hamlet* the expression 'all the Region Kites' (II ii 574) may be understood as 'all the kites of the region', in which *Region* has adopted the possessive form without *-s*. One might add here that when words do have a final *-s* it is not easy to decide whether they are possessive or not, particularly when a participle follows. This is because the use of the apostrophe was not well developed by this period. Thus when Hotspur says 'I then, all-smarting, with my wounds being cold' (*1H4* I iii 49), it is not possible to tell whether *wounds* is modifier or head, and if the former whether there is one wound or several. When two words occur in the modifier slot it is possible, as we have seen, that one is an intensifier to the other or that both are independent modifiers to the head. When the first of these is a word like *high*, *well* or *all*, it is customary to hyphenate it to the following word so that there are many compounds in Shakespeare like 'high-battled' (*Ant.* III xiii 29 Folio reads 'hye battel'd'), 'well-desired' (*Oth.* II i 202, Folio reads 'well desir'd') and 'all-lycenc'd (*Lear* I iv 199). However, other comparable words like *most* and *very* are rarely presented as compounds. Even some examples of the three words referred to are treated as independent modifiers. Thus we find the line:

Noble, Couragious, high vnmatchable (*Ant.* II iii 21)

with *high* as a separate modifier, though *high-unmatchable* would seem a reasonable interpretation. At other times the hyphen may conceal other potential readings. In the *Comedy of Errors* the Folio line 'Sleeping or waking, mad or well aduisde' (II ii 212) is often punctuated *well-advis'd* today which suggests that *mad* is contrasted with *well-advis'd*, though it is quite possible to think that *mad* and *well* are both intensifiers to *aduisde* for *mad* was a perfectly acceptable adverbial form. Similarly in *Antony and Cleopatra* the hyphen taken over from the Folio in the line:

I will be trebble-sinewed, hearted, breath'd (III xiii 178)

conceals the link of *trebble* with *hearted* and *breath'd*.

Since a substantive can fill a modifier slot it is not easy to tell whether in many instances it is a modifier or whether one should accept that there are two co-ordinate nominal groups. When Hamlet says 'Oh what a Rogue and Pesant slaue am I' (*Ham.* II ii 543), it is possible to assume that he is a rogue as well as a boorish slave or that he is a roguish and boorish slave. Similarly *geering* in 'the geering and disdain'd contempt' (*1H4* I iii 183) can be understood as head or modifier. Probably in the theatre most listeners interpret the lines of the song in *As You Like It*:

Heere shall he see no enemie,
But Winter and rough Weather (II v 39–41)

as though *Winter* and *Weather* were two separate heads of their own nominal groups. However, the occurrence later in the same play of the expression *thou winter winde* (II vii 174) in another song shows that *winter* could readily be taken as a modifier in such contexts. Probably there is only one nominal group in the first song which has the meaning 'boisterous, wintry weather', which is indeed the sole enemy. However, the occurrence of adjectives in the second modifier slot will make it increasingly difficult for modern readers to understand the substantive in the first slot as a modifier. In *King Richard the Second* when Mowbray calls Bolingbroke 'A recreant, and most degenerate Traitor' (I i 144), most modern readers are likely to take *recreant* as parallel to *Traitor* rather than to *most degenerate*, though the latter might seem the better interpretation.

An indulgence in modifiers is usually considered part of poetic, or even a too poetic, style. Certainly they were liberally employed in the Elizabethan period and they are more characteristic of Shakespeare's early than of his mature style. They encourage the conceit in which the modifier and the head may apparently belong to different registers – and the immediate juxtaposition of two opposites throws the contrast into special relief. A good example occurs in *Romeo and Juliet*:

> Why then, O brawling loue, O louing hate,
> O any thing, of nothing first created:
> O heauie lightnesse, serious vanity,
> Mishapen Chaos of welseeing formes,
> Feather of lead, bright smoake, cold fire, sicke health. (I i 174–8)

In this quotation it may be seen how easily the contrast is made between modifier and head as in *heauie lightnesse*; such a contrast is much less marked when there is a qualifier as in *feather of lead*. It is also characteristic that the modifier plus head group readily contrasts with other groups of the same structure; often two such groups fill the two halves of a line as in *O heauie lightnesse, serious vanity*. This type of structure is one that occurs readily in Shakespeare's plays and helps to create the rhythm of his lines. It helps to provide the structure of such lines as 'Say the firme Roman to great Egypt sends' (*Ant.* I v 43), and it was a useful tool for Shakespeare and other Elizabethans in writing blank verse. The contrast of nominal groups consisting of head and qualifier is usually much less obvious, for qualifiers do not necessarily have the same structure. Thus when Enobarbus says that 'we did sleepe day out of countenaunce: and made the night light with drinking' (*Ant.* II ii 181–2), it is clear that there is parallelism between *out of countenaunce* and *with drinking*, but it comes much less pat than with modifiers. Similarly in *Cymbeline* when Belarius says:

'Tis wonder
That an inuisible instinct should frame them
To Royalty vnlearn'd, Honor vntaught,
Ciuility not seene from other: valour
That wildely growes in them (IV ii 177–81)

there is a parallelism between *Royalty vnlearn'd* and *Honor vntaught* which is soon lost in the other nominal groups which have lengthier qualifiers. When a modifier plus head and a head plus qualifier are linked, it needs at least one word of similar or identical form to make the parallelism explicit, as in 'and things outward Do draw the inward quality after them' (*Ant.* III xiii 32–3), where the repetition of the *-ward* is sufficient to point the link. However, it appears that Shakespeare grew tired of the too easy parallelism of the modifer plus head groups, for this structure is much more common in his earlier plays than in the later ones. No doubt he found the structure too obvious as he worked towards subtler and more demanding rhythms in his later plays.

An interesting aspect of a nominal group like *great Egypt* is that modifiers can readily be attached to a proper noun whether it refers to a person or place. If it is a person it needs no title like *Sir* or determiner like *the*. This ability of Elizabethan English for a modifier to be attached to almost any name was clearly useful to Shakespeare in such plays as the historical ones, since there names occur frequently. It enabled him to use a variety of names and also to modify them to produce variation. This ability suggests that in Elizabethan English the distance between proper and other nouns to which we are accustomed today was not as noticeable then. There was little formal or qualitative difference between *great queen* and *great Egypt* as appellations for Cleopatra.

As we have already seen in discussing *brothers dead loue*, the order of modifiers in Shakespearian English is fluid. In Modern English there is a preferred order which expresses the direct relationship between the various parts of the nominal group. This does not apply to Shakespeare who has many phrases like 'masculine vsurp'd attyre' (*TN* V i 242) which in Modern English is more likely to appear as 'usurped masculine attire'. It may be part of this freedom which allows the modifier in Shakespearian English to consist of a phrase which would today appear only as a qualifier. In:

> O that it could be prou'd,
> That some Night-tripping-Faiery, had exchang'd,
> In Cradle-clothes, our Children where they lay (*1H4* I i 86–8)

the *In Cradle-clothes* is in the modifier position, though it would today occur only after the head. This example is particularly interesting for it illustrates a further feature of the nominal group, which is that the qualifier which follows the head need not refer back to the head but to the modifier, or even, as here, to part of the modifier. The *where they lay* refers not to the head *Children* but to *Cradle*, which is the first half of the compound modifier.

This is an extreme example of a type which is perhaps better known in such forms as the 'Arch-bishops Grace of Yorke' (*1H4* III ii 119) rather than the 'Archbishop of York's Grace', for this type of possessive form is familiar from a variety of old titles of literary works like *The Wife's Tale of Bath*. It is also not uncommon for a phrase dependent upon an adjective to be in the qualifier position even though the adjective appears in the modifier slot. Hence we find 'Bring forth that fatall Schreechowle to our house' (*3H6* II vi 56) with the *to our house* separated from the *fatall*, and 'Nor scarre that whiter skin of hers, then Snow' (*Oth.* V ii 4) with the *then Snow* separated from *whiter*. A slightly more complicated example is 'The perturb'd Court For my being absent?' (*Cym.* III iv 104–5) in which some editors put a comma after *Court* and some, following the Folio, omit it. In the latter case the editors presumably relate the *perturb'd* directly to *For my being absent*, but in the former reading a different grammatical relationship may be intended though the phrase is not usually explained. The qualifier may be a nominal group itself in a loose grammatical relationship to the modifier as in 'With this Slaues Offall, bloudy: a Bawdy villaine' (*Ham.* II ii 575). Here many modern editors read 'Slave's offal, bloody, bawdy villain', in which the *bloody, bawdy villain* is a qualifier to the modifier *slave's* rather than to the head *offal*. Other editors conceal this relationship by putting a fullstop after *offal* and starting a new verbless sentence with *bloody*. This seems an unnecessary editorial intervention in the punctuation motivated by a reluctance to accept this type of qualifier. Yet there are many comparable examples, as:

at *Maluolio's* suite,
A Gentleman, and follower of my Ladies; (*TN* V i 268–9)

and:

True, who beares hard
His Brothers death at *Bristow*, the Lord *Scroope*.
(*1H4* I iii 270–1)

Even when there is a determiner such as a possessive adjective rather than a modifier in the nominal group, the qualifier may still refer to that rather than to the head. In:

But iealousie, what might befall your trauell [*Folio* rrauell]
Being skillesse in these parts (*TN* III iii 8–9)

the whole second line is a qualifier which refers to a *you* which has to be understood in the *your*, the determiner to *trauell*. Similarly in:

What foolish boldnesse brought thee to their mercies,
Whom thou in termes so bloudie, and so deere
Hast made thine enemies? (*TN* V i 64–6)

the second and third lines form a qualifier in the nominal group, which refers back to a *they* which is understood from the determiner *their*.

Although this type of construction is accepted in its simpler manifestations, more complicated examples may be misunderstood and even emended out of existence. A passage in *Twelfth Night* in the Folio reads as follows:

For folly that he wisely shewes, is fit;
But wisemens folly falne, quite taint their wit. (III i 64–5)

The last line has usually been considered unintelligible by modern editors who have suggested a variety of emendations, of which the most popular is *wise men folly-fall'n*, as in the Arden and Alexander editions. However, this emendation destroys the comparison between the folly of the fool and that of the wise men. We have seen that a modifier which is a possessive often has the qualifier agreeing with it instead of with the head of the nominal group. It would be quite possible therefore to understand *falne* to refer back to *wisemens* so that the nominal group means 'the folly of fallen wise men', which makes acceptable sense in the context. This merely leaves the problem of the apparently plural form of the verb *taint* which has a singular subject – a lack of congruence not without parallel in Shakespeare.

Qualifiers can be introduced by a relative pronoun or by none at all. In Shakespeare both forms can be found side by side, a construction which is not normal in Modern English. In the following passage:

> A Sonne, who is the Theame of Honors tongue;
> Among'st a Groue, the very straightest Plant,
> Who is sweet Fortunes Minion, and her Pride (*1H4* I i 81–3)

there are three qualifiers, but only two of them are introduced by *who*. The intermediate one is a free-standing nominal group only loosely linked to the head. In Modern English it is possible to omit the relative pronoun only when it is the object complement of the verb in the qualifier, as in 'the boy I love' rather than 'the boy whom I love'. In Elizabethan English it was possible to omit it also when it was the subject of the qualifier as in 'My Father had a Daughter lou'd a man' i.e. a daughter who loved (*TN* II iv 106). Some of these can easily confuse readers who are relatively unfamiliar with Elizabethan English, as is true of:

> And bring him out, that is but Womans Sonne,
> Can trace me in the tedious wayes of Art. (*1H4* III i 47–8)

Here a *who* has to be understood before *Can* to relate the last line as a qualifier to *him*. Naturally, it can also happen that the relative has an uncertain antecedent or one which has to be extrapolated from some part of the preceding nominal group. In:

> This is his Vncles teaching. This is Worcester
> Maleuolent to you in all Aspects:
> Which makes him prune himselfe . . . (*1H4* I i 96–8)

the *which* presumably refers to Worcester's malevolence which is understood from the word *maleuolent*. These types of omission allow Shakespeare to create his elliptical style.

The order in a nominal group in Shakespeare's English has much greater freedom than we are accustomed to today, and a mark of that freedom is the ability to detach part of the nominal group from the immediate environment of the head. There are many examples of what may be called 'hanging phrases' in Shakespeare, particularly those which contain a participle. Such detached phrases can either precede or follow the head. As examples of anticipation consider:

> Heere in the streets, desperate of shame and state,
> In priuate brabble did we apprehend him (*TN* V i 58–9)

where the *desperate of shame and state* anticipates the *him* of the following line. It may readily be appreciated that such anticipation could cause confusion as to the correct interpretation of the passage since a different head, *we*, comes between the detached phrase and its head. The antecedent phrase may have as its referent a part of the nominal group which is not the head in much the same way as we have already seen with qualifiers. Thus in:

> Comming from *Sardis*, on our former Ensigne
> Two mighty Eagles fell (*JC* V i 79–80)

the initial phrase has to be understood as agreeing with a *we* understood from the *our* rather than with *Ensigne* or even *Eagles*. This is an unusual example, for generally an initial detached phrase of this type tends to refer to the object complement. Perhaps the best known example is in *Hamlet*:

> It's giuen out, that sleeping in mine Orchard,
> A Serpent stung me . . . . (I v 35–6)

Such phrases may also follow the head. In the following example:

> For he that brought them, in the very heate
> And pride of their contention, did take horse,
> Vncertaine of the issue any way. (*1H4* I i 59–61)

the final line refers back to *he* in the first line. Another example occurs somewhat later in the same play:

And on my face he turn'd an eye of death,
Trembling euen at the name of *Mortimer*. (*1H4* I iii 143–4)

Many of these hanging phrases contain participles, which are among the more difficult aspects of Shakespeare's language to pin down grammatically. Participles were originally parts of verbs and they can preserve some of the properties of verbs in Shakespeare's usage. An example of this is his ability to modify a participial head with an adverbial modifier as in 'To plague thee, for thy foule mis-leading me' (*3H6* V i 97) where *foule* has to be understood as an adverbial modifier meaning 'foully' even though it comes between the determiner *thy* and the head *misleading*. This type of modifier is not retained in Modern English. The second example of the verbal nature of a participial head is still found today, though it is now much restricted in usage. This is the ability of a participial head to take an object as in *the seeing these effects* (*Cym* v 25), where in Modern English it would be more common to insert a preposition after the head to make the following phrase more of a qualifier.

A feature of Elizabethan English is the much wider role of participles in the nominal group than is usual today. Some of these features reflect grammatical arrangements which we have already noted. In these lines in *Cymbeline*:

A Foolish Suitor to a Wedded Lady,
That hath her Husband banish'd (I vi 2–3)

the *banish'd* might readily be understood by modern students to be part of the verbal group *hath banished*. In fact it is the qualifier to the head *Husband*, for the lady in question has a banished husband and has not herself banished him. The participle can act as a modifier in a way which would not be acceptable today except in set phrases. In *Cymbeline* we find 'admir'd Successe', i.e. success which is admired (I i 32) and 'In these fear'd hope' (II iv 6) where the *hope* is often amended to *hopes* by modern editors because of the unfamiliar construction. In many cases the participle possibly forms part of an elliptical construction as in 'Of one perswaded well of' (*Cym.* II iv 132), which means 'of one who is held in high esteem'. It is possible to take *perswaded* as a qualifier to *one* either absolutely or as part of a relative clause in which the relative pronoun has been omitted. Another example, this time from *The Merchant of Venice*, indicates the same ambiguity. In 'a diamond gone cost me two thousand ducats' (III i 72) it is possible to take *gone* as the verb with a part of the auxiliary "to be" missing and then it will be necessary to understand a missing relative pronoun before *cost.* The sense would then be 'A diamond is gone which cost me . . .'. It is, however, possible to take *gone* as a qualifier so that the sentence means 'A lost diamond cost me . . .'. This kind of participial arrangement is one of the means Shakespeare used to link different parts of his sentence together and these will be elaborated upon further in a later chapter.

Participles, perhaps because of their verbal origins, also have a passive sense when used in a nominal group. In 'to whose feeling sorrowes' (*WT* IV ii 8), the sorrows are those which are deeply felt. Similarly Antony's 'all-obeying breath' (*Ant.* III xiii 77) is breath which everything obeys. In *Twelfth Night* a 'vouchsafed eare' (III i 86) is one which is granted. In the qualifier slot we may note such examples as 'How scap'd I killing, when I crost you so?' (*JC* IV iii 147) where *killing* has the passive sense of being killed.

The other major part of the nominal group is the determiner which precedes the modifier and in Modern English consists of a mutually exclusive set of words like *a*, *the*, *his* and *this.* In Modern English some determiners have two possible forms though these are usually found in complementary distribution so that they cannot be used interchangeably in any given context. Thus *an* is used before vowels and initial *h*, and *a* is used in other environments. In Shakespearian English the determiners are not mutually exclusive since expressions like 'An Instrument of this your calling backe' (*Oth.* IV ii 46) occur in which *this* and *your*, which could not both be present in Modern English, are found as determiners to *calling.* This type of expression is found today only archaically as in the biblical *these my sins.* Even in Elizabethan times the use of two determiners was not common, and it seems to have been used for emphasis.

Emphasis and euphony are important aspects in the use of determiners as they are of pronouns in general. Thus the variation between *my* and *mine* was not determined in Elizabethan times by structural constraints as in Modern English; it was a matter of emphasis. The *mine* form was more usually found before vowels, but it may be replaced by *my* when the determiner carries stress. Words like *ear* and *eye* would more frequently be preceded by *mine*, but in the following examples from *A Midsummer Night's Dream my* is used. In 'My eare should catch your voice, my eye, your eye' (I i 188) the two instances of *my* are parallel and contrast with *your* in each case. They carry more emphasis than usual and so it is appropriate to call attention to this through the form *my*. When Helena says to Hermione 'Haue you not set *Lysander*, as in scorne To follow me, and praise my eies and face?' (III ii 222–3), she stresses the *my* because she feels that Hermione has set Lysander on to mock her particular form of beauty, for the two girls are depicted as strikingly different in their appearance. So in reading Shakespeare it is important to pay attention to these indications of emphasis which help to indicate a speaker's tone of voice.

Pronominal forms in Elizabethan English are very close to those found today, though there are some important differences. The possessive form of *it*, for example, is *his* and this can lead to ambiguity or misunderstanding. When *his* is used to refer to some abstract quality or a geographical feature, it is not clear whether Shakespeare is using personification allegory or whether he is merely following the normal grammatical conventions of his day. Allegory is clearly involved in statements such as:

> Vertue it selfe, of Vice must pardon begge,
> Yea courb, and woe, for leaue to do him good (*Ham.* III iv 154–5)

where the *him* instead of *it* indicates that Shakespeare has here appropriated the allegorical stance of the older morality plays. Hence when he uses *his* in such sentences as:

> The Southerne winde
> Doth play the Trumpet to his purposes,
> And by his hollow whistling in the Leaues,
> Fortels a Tempest, and a blust'ring day (*1H4* V i 3–6)

it is possible that he is personifying the wind. On balance this is perhaps less likely than that he was merely using the normal grammatical form; and one may well think that the average Elizabethan playgoer would have taken *his* as common usage rather than as an indication of allegory. Nevertheless editors and critics do sometimes read into these forms support for a particular allegorical interpretation. On occasion a reading of this type may be implied, though it is not explicitly stated. In *King John* the following lines are spoken by Constance:

> I will instruct my sorrowes to bee proud,
> For greefe is proud, and makes his owner stoope.
>
> (III i 68–9)

The Arden editor, Professor Honigmann, adds a note 'Shakespeare depicts Constance bowed down by the pride which Grief is said to possess.'[6] We can only assume that the capital *G* of his Grief in this note means that he accepted that Shakespeare was here personifying grief, even though he keeps the Folio's lower case letter in his own text. Small details such as this may readily convince a student that *his* is used to indicate personification by Shakespeare.

Nouns are distinguished today by their ability to take an indefinite article or not; those that can are known as count nouns because they can be counted, *a cat*: *two cats*, and those that cannot are known as non-count nouns, for *cattle* accepts no indefinite article and cannot have a plural either. Proper nouns have many of the characteristics of non-count nouns, though they are normally considered to form a separate class. As we have already noted, the difference between proper nouns and count nouns was small in Elizabethan English; and the same goes for the difference between count and non-count nouns. Many nouns that today would take an article can frequently be found without one. Examples such as:

> So longest Way shall haue the longest Moanes (*R2* V i 90)

and

> And with no lesse Nobility of Loue,
> Then that which deerest Father beares his Sonne
>
> (*Ham.* I ii 110–11)

are common enough. By the same token non-count nouns which today cannot have a plural form are often found in the plural in Shakespearian English. Hence we find such examples as 'Reuenges burne in them' (*Macb.* V ii 3) and 'Which giue some soyle (perhaps) to my Behauiours' (*JC* I ii 42). From a grammatical point of view the difference between the various types of noun is not easy to categorise. This close association between different nouns may account for the apparent inability to separate some modifiers and adverbs which have become more specialised in meaning today.

Words like *many*, *much*, *more* are used in a wider range of grammatical construction in Shakespeare, perhaps because their specialised meaning today is dependent upon a formal distinction between different classes of noun.

It may be this same grammatical freedom which accounts for the instances of such expressions as *a many men* and *a few men* met with in Shakespeare's works. In *As You Like It* we find 'a many merry men' (I i 105) and in *King John* 'a many thousand warlike French' (IV ii 199). Sometimes words like *many* are placed before the *a* as in the nature of a pre-determiner, though in such cases they appear to have an adverbial rather than an adjectival sense. When Leontes says in *The Winter's Tale*:

> and haue (in vaine) said many
> A prayer vpon her graue (V iii 140–1)

it is likely that *many* has the sense 'on many occasions'. It is parallel to the adverbial meaning of *poore* in 'it was vpon this fashion bequeathed me by will, but poore a thousand Crownes' (*AYL* I i 2). It is possible on occasion for these two constructions to be united as in *King John* where the Bastard Faulconbridge says:

> But many a many foot of Land the worse (I i 183)

The Arden editor notes that '*many a many* is unique here in Shakespeare, typical of Faulconbridge's loose language'[7]. This interpretation, however, is not satisfactory, for uniqueness in Shakespeare is not the same as loose language. The two halves of the construction are readily paralleled from other passages in Shakespeare and the phrase cannot be interpreted as an example of incorrect language or loose style, even assuming that such a concept had any relevance for Shakespeare and his audience. Indeed, the repetition of *many* might well have been thought of as a verbal play which attracted admiration rather than criticism. It is possible to interpret the line as 'But often worse off by many acres of land.'

Finally a few words may be included about those personal pronouns which can stand as the head of a nominal group. These pronouns were originally inflected through several cases, and some of those inflections, e.g. *I* and *me*, still survive. In Elizabethan English the distinction between the cases was blurred, and it seems that cases could often be used more for emphasis than for grammatical propriety. This position may have been occasioned by the fall of the original dative case, meaning 'to' *or* 'for', which led to confusion in certain constructions particularly the imperative one. When in *Macbeth* we find 'take thee that too' (II i 5), it is possible to interpret *thee* as an old dative meaning 'to you', though it might seem as though it ought to be the subject of *take* and so appear as *thou.* This use of an object case where the subject should be found does occur in many instances, as when Claudio says 'Stand thee by Frier' (*Ado* IV i 22), for in this example an interpretation of *thee* as a former dative is not possible. It is clear that *thee* and *thou* could interchange. The same is true of *ye* (the subject form) and *you* (the object form), as is apparent in 'Therein, yee Gods, you make the weake most strong' (*JC* I iii 91) in which both *yee* and *you* are used to refer to the gods. The explanation may well be that *you* and *thou* were considered more emphatic than *ye* and *thee.* Naturally after imperatives an unemphatic form was in order; and we today have eliminated the pronoun altogether because we consider it unnecessary. In the example from *Julius Caesar* the occurrence of *yee* before Gods is understandably unemphatic, but the *you* afterwards is used to stress their power. Emphasis is part of euphony, because it will be possible to adjust the weight given to a particular word to enhance the rhythm of a line. It may also be emphasis which accounts for the use of, for example, *she* for *her* in examples which many people still consider a mark of ungrammaticality in Shakespeare. When Othello says to Emilia 'Yes, you haue seene *Cassio*, and she together' (*Oth.* IV ii 3), the *she* is much more explicit and dramatic than *her* would be.

It is possible to push this concept of emphasis too far, but it is certainly one which should be taken into account as it enables a reader to understand the attitudes of the various characters. The same is true of the use of *thou/thee* where one might have expected *ye/you.* The former were used as a mark of intimacy or as a sign of contempt, and as such they are also emphatic. Examples of this use have been given in the Introduction and no further ones will be provided here. As in all instances of unexpected cases of pronouns, the context has to be taken into consideration to see whether Shakespeare was exploiting the conditions of the language to draw attention to a particular relationship. The choice between variables of this kind is not one which we have today and so it is easy to overlook the emphasis intended. Yet a student should not assume that all examples of unexpected pronoun forms are significant; the context and other linguistic markers will usually help to point the way.

The nominal group is that part of the structure of English which conveys the most meaning and exhibits the greatest variety. If this is true of Modern English, it is even more true for Elizabethan English. Shakespeare uses the nominal group flexibly, though only some indication of its wide range has been given in this chapter. It is the principal vehicle for his meaning and it encapsulates much of the metaphor and imagery. Often, however, it is not the choice of words in the nominal group that is so important as their arrangement. The syntax of the nominal group is always worth paying attention to, for it contributes to the emphasis, euphony and rhythm of Shakespeare's lines - and these are all aspects which he valued more than simple meaning.

5 The Verbal Group

After the nominal group the most important group in a sentence is the verbal group. Like the nominal group it consists of three elements known as the auxiliary, the verb and the extension, for these three occur in that order in the group although the verb is its only essential part. Thus if there is a nominal group subject like *The man*, it can be followed by a verbal group such as *should drink up*, in which *should* is the auxiliary, *drink* the verb, and *up* the extension. Unlike the nominal group, the verbal group cannot be indefinitely expanded. In Elizabethan English it is most usual to find that each part of the verbal group consists of only one word each, though longer examples may be found. Certainly the extensive auxiliaries found in Modern English such as *might have been being (roasted)* are not found in Elizabethan English, where an auxiliary of more than two parts is rare. In Modern English these auxiliaries help to provide variety of tenses among other things. In Elizabethan English this variety was either not found or had to be expressed through other mechanisms, such as the subjunctive or the adverbial group. Consequently each verb form in Shakespeare's English has potentially a wider range of meaning than its Modern English counterpart, though for the most part the verbs do not carry as much information as they do today. This makes them simpler and stronger.

By Shakespeare's time the verb had not stabilised in form or function. The latter may be illustrated by the ambiguous borderline between the nominal and the verbal groups which is provided by the participles. In some of Shakespeare's more elliptical writing it is sometimes difficult to tell what function the participle plays. The former arose from the history of the verb in English. Originally the English verb consisted of only two tenses, a present and a past, in either indicative or subjunctive mood. It was the decay of the subjunctive which hastened the development of auxiliaries. Furthermore, the inflectional endings of the different persons in each tense were not uniform throughout English dialects and this led to variety in those endings in London English. Particularly noticeable at Shakespeare's time was the variety between the *-(e)s* and *-(e)th* endings of the third person of the present indicative. One could write *goes* or *goeth*, a useful expedient for poets since the former was monosyllabic and the latter bisyllabic. Furthermore, each tense was expressed originally only through one form. This form has been supplemented by the so-called expanded forms, so that instead of saying simply *goes* or *goeth*, one can now also say *does go* and *is going*. Expanded forms are found in Shakespeare's writings, though not frequently. In addition English has two types of verb, one which forms its preterite by adding *-(e)d* to the stem and the other which forms the preterite and past participle by changing the root vowel of the stem as in a series like *ride – rode – ridden*. The latter verbs were more frequent in earlier English and exhibited a wider range of vowel changes. In the Elizabethan period the vowels were being regrouped with the effect that there was considerable flexibility in the range of forms available to many verbs. It was possible to have weak and strong preterities for the same verb such as *climbed* and *clomb*, and to have different vowels in the preterite or past participle of strong verbs such as *he has write*, *he has wrote* or *he has written*.

This variety raises the question whether there were grammatical differences between the various forms or whether their use was governed by stylistic criteria alone. The latter seems to have been the case. As already suggested, the usefulness of differing forms of the present indicative in *-(e)s* and *-(e)th* lay in their varying syllabic lengths. Other forms could be useful since they had different vowels and so were able to be rhymed with different words. However, these differences were not simply free variants which could be used to meet the dictates of rhyme or metre. Some at least appear to represent different stylistic registers. This applies particularly to the expanded tense with *do*. Today *do* is used in certain functional situations such as negative and interrogative sentences and its use need not imply any stylistic significance. It was, however, originally employed for emphasis and at this period it retained much of this force. Even so, it had its usefulness from a metrical point of view, since the *do* form could provide a different rhythm in the sentence and an extra syllable. Its use in some instances in Shakespeare may be merely to provide the necessary metre in the blank verse. When an expanded form is found side by side with an unexpanded one as in:

> and *Charles* the Great
> Subdu'd the Saxons, and did seat the French
> Beyond the Riuer Sala (*H5* I ii 61–3)

it is reasonable to assume that the two forms are used without stylistic distinction. Yet the origin of the *do* form in emphatic sentences meant that it was often used to imply a different register.

The *do* form is often found in more inflated language, as though the circumlocution added more gravity and weight to the utterance. It is not without significance that the player king and queen in *Hamlet* use several *do* forms in their language, since that is marked by a pompous and pretentious level of style. Examples like:

> Since loue our hearts, and *Hymen* did our hands
> Vnite comutuall (*Ham.* III ii 154–5)

and

> I do beleeue you. Think what now you speak:
> But what we do determine, oft we breake (*Ham.* III ii 181–2)

underline this use of *do*. The last example is particularly interesting since the *do* forms are often found in official or high style, and their occurrence may help to underline the tone of certain speeches. Thus in the opening scene in *King Lear* it is particularly common in many of Lear's speeches, which express official attitudes or curses. Hence we find such examples as 'Which of you doth loue vs most' (l. 50), 'I doe inuest you ioyntly' (l. 129), 'Fiue dayes we do allot thee' (l. 173), and 'When she was deare to vs, we did hold her so' (l. 196). Many of these utterances have a ponderousness supported by other verbal features to be considered shortly. Only Kent has a similar *do* form, which is significantly used when he protests Cordelia's love for Lear:

> Thy yongest Daughter do's not loue thee least (l. 151).

Goneril and Regan do not use the *do* forms when they protest their love for Lear, and this may imply some lack of weight in their claims.

The absence of *do* forms in negative and interrogative sentences may make their appearance in ordinary declarative sentences more powerful than they would otherwise be. The use of *do* forms should probably be considered together with examples of *has/hath* with the past participle to express the perfect and of auxiliaries with the infinitive. Such verb forms are longer and so perhaps weightier than the simple forms, and they may add an element of dignity to the language. The perfect is usually used of an action in the past which still has present effect, whereas the preterite is used of an action completed in the past. However, this distinction is not rigidly adhered to in Elizabethan English as seems to be the case in *King Lear.* It may not be entirely chance which leads blunt Kent to use the preterite as in:

'My life I neuer held but as pawne' (I i 154),

whereas Lear and the courtly France and Burgundy use the perfect, as in

'I craue no more then hath your Highnesse offer'd' (I i 194).

The role of auxiliaries is a matter to be discussed presently, though one may say now that the use of some auxiliary forms was more a matter of style than meaning. It is noticeable that in this scene in *King Lear* there are many examples of auxiliaries which help again to set a more formal tone to the proceedings. Thus when Cordelia says:

Happily when I shall wed,
That Lord, whose hand must take my plight, shall carry
Halfe my loue with him, halfe my Care, and Dutie
(I i 99–101)

the use of *shall* and *must* is hardly necessary for the meaning of the passage, for the former verbal group might be expressed more usually as *wed* and the latter as *takes* or *will take.* The auxiliaries used add dignity, formality and a sense of official activity to the scene. They imply a certain assertiveness within a diplomatic framework, and in this way they contribute with the other verb forms to the tone of the scene, in which declamation and statements of position are prominent.

Since reference has been made to the auxiliaries, it may be appropriate to consider the form and function of the subjunctive which was gradually being replaced at this time by various auxiliaries. Originally the present and preterite tenses had had morphologically distinct subjunctive forms. With the decay of inflections, the distinctions had largely been lost except in the second and third person singular of the present subjunctive, where the subjunctive had endingless forms as compared with the indicative endings in *-est* and *-es/eth*. However, as the second singular form was itself in decay, this meant that the primary distinction lay in the third person singular; even today *Long live the Queen* is distinguished from *She lives there*. In addition the verb *to be* had distinctive subjunctive forms, as is still true to some extent, for we can say *If I were you* rather than *If I was you*. Although the subjunctive was in decline in the Elizabethan period, it was still used far more widely than today for it had considerable vitality and usefulness.

The subjunctive could be used in either main or subordinate clauses. In the former it usually implies a wish, threat or command. In many instances modern readers are not likely to be in doubt as to the meaning, even if the concept of a subjunctive is unknown to them. When in *Macbeth* Lennox says 'better health Attend his Maiesty' (III iv 120–1), few are likely to be in any doubt about the expression of a wish. Examples like 'As much good stay with thee, as go with mee' (*R2* I ii 57) are less easy to disentangle with its two subjunctives; the sense is 'May as much good remain here with you as I hope will go with me'. The unfamiliarity of the subjunctive form may cause some uncertainty either when the verb is somewhat unusual or when the endingless inflection might be confused with some other part of speech such as an imperative. The former may occur when the verb has been formed from functional shift or when it is a verb which is no longer current today. When in *The Winter's Tale* a lady says of the Queen:

She is spread of late
Into a goodly Bulke (good time encounter her.) (II i 19–20)

the strangeness of the verb *encounter* and the subjunctive form may perplex many modern students as to the meaning of the line. The same could easily apply to a sentence like:

> Some light-foot friend post to ye Duke of Norfolk
> (*R3* IV iv 440)

where *post* is in the subjunctive indicating a wish. The latter may occur in sentences where the idea of a wish may not at first be obvious and where alternative interpretations may be sought, particularly as the forms of the verb were unstable at the time and so it might be easy to assume that a final *-s* was missing. Thus in *The Second Part of King Henry the Sixth* a sentence like the following occurs:

> Who loues the King, and will imbrace his pardon,
> Fling vp his cap, and say, God saue his Maiesty . . . .
> (IV viii 13–14)

Here it is possible that many might wish to take *fling* as an indicative verb indicating a command rather than a subjunctive implying a wish. Later in the same scene when Cade says 'My sword make way for me, for heere is no staying', it may well be that many students would also try to understand *make* as an imperative or as an indicative form without *-s*.

Occasionally a verb in the main clause may be in the subjunctive implying a difference in thought or estimation from the use of the indicative. This is particularly the case with the verb 'to dare'. This distinction can be seen very clearly in *The Tempest* where Caliban is discussing with Stephano and Trinculo how to get the better of Prospero. Caliban says to Stephano:

> If thy Greatnesse will
> Reuenge it on him, (for I know thou dar'st)
> But this Thing dare not. (III ii 50–2)

Here the *this Thing* is Trinculo. The first example of the verb *dar'st* is clearly indicative, and the second *dare* is subjunctive. The meaning is that Stephano does dare (*indicative*) to tackle Prospero, but Trinculo would not dare approach him under any circumstances (*subjunctive*). This is an important shade of meaning which Shakespeare is able to convey through the different verbal moods.

In the preterite the subjunctive usually has the same form as the indicative and so it has to be recognised from the context, although it was possible to express the preterite subjunctive through the past tense of the verb 'to have' or the subjunctive preterite of the verb 'to be', which has the distinctive form *were*. It was also possible to use an auxiliary with the infinitive. The existence of these latter forms may make it easier to misinterpret those examples of the subjunctive formed in the older ways as the indicative, for readers may assume that all single verb forms are indicative. There may also be subtle differences in meaning between the simple and expanded forms of the subjunctive. In an example from *The Merchant of Venice* the occurrence of the conditional with *if* makes the mood of *stood* in the main clause clear:

> But if my Father had not scanted me, . . .
> Your selfe (renowned Prince) than stood as faire. (II i 17–20)

The sense is 'would have stood', though the use of the simple *stood* rather than the expanded *had stood* may imply more definiteness in the statement as if Portia meant 'you would undoubtedly have stood'. A similar shade of meaning may be found in an example from *Othello*, where the presence of the subjunctive may not even be suspected by many modern students:

> Preferment goes by Letter, and affection,
> And not by old gradation, where each second
> Stood Heire to'th'first. (I i 36–8)

Here Iago may imply that the second should naturally and by the proper course of nature succeed the first; there may be a subtlety of meaning not immediately apparent in the use of the subjunctive in Shakespeare.

Examples of the subjunctive with an auxiliary are common enough, though the range of auxiliary used is wider than today with *could*, *would*, *might* and *must* all being used. Sometimes the main verb may have an auxiliary, which seems logically unnecessary, and the auxiliary in this case may simply have been attracted by the one in the subordinate clause. Thus when Don Pedro in *Much Ado About Nothing* says of Benedick 'I could wish he would modestly examine himselfe' (II iii 190), he means he wishes Benedick would examine himself. Most examples of the subjunctive with an auxiliary are unlikely to confuse a modern reader, though some may strike him as unusual for each auxiliary has a wider range of meaning than today.

In certain subordinate clauses the subjunctive is used, because its function is to express something which is not necessarily true or which is not known to be true. Thus it is usual to find it in conditional clauses introduced by *if*, which naturally express something which is not factual, and after verbs expressing hope, thought or fear. Elizabethan English would normally use such constructions as 'I hope he be in loue' (*Ado* III ii 15), for the verb *hope* implies expectation, but no certainty. Nevertheless, examples of the indicative form are found occasionally after such verbs, though it is difficult to decide how to interpret them. On the one hand, they may simply be examples of the gradual decay of the subjunctive. On the other hand, they may defeat the expectation of the subjunctive and so imply that although the character only hopes or fears something is true, what they hope or fear is indeed real. When Desdemona says to Othello:

I hope my Noble Lord esteemes me honest (*Oth.* IV ii 66)

we would expect *esteem* (subjunctive) rather than *esteemes* (indicative). Her use of the indicative may imply that she is indeed honest. Similarly when the messenger in *Macbeth* comes to warn Lady Macduff that she should flee from her house, he says:

I doubt some danger do's approach you neerely (IV ii 66)

As soon as he leaves the stage the murderers of Lady Macduff and her children come on, and so the messenger's indicative *do's* where the subjunctive *do* would be expected announces that the impending danger he fears is real.

As already noted the subjunctive is used in conditional clauses after such conjunctions as *if*. However, conditions can be expressed through inversion of subject and verb rather than through a conjunction. In such cases the verb will be in the subjunctive, though as so often the form of the subjunctive is not always different from that of the indicative. A good example of this is found in *The Merchant of Venice* where Portia says 'Liue thou, I liue' (III ii 61), that is 'If you should live, I will live'. The first form *liue* is clearly in the subjunctive, for the indicative form would be *liuest.* This type of subjunctive is not uncommon in Shakespeare and helps to give many passages a pregnancy and urgency which would be missing with the more cumbersome *if* construction. This can be seen in Iago's

Liue *Rodorigo*,
He calles me to a restitution large
Of Gold, and Iewels . . . . (*Oth.* V i 14–16)

The subjunctive is also used in subordinate clauses to imply purpose whether that clause is introduced with a *that* or not. In the following example the second *meet* is the subjunctive: 'Therefore 'tis meet, *Achilles* meet not *Hector*' (*Troil.* I iii 358). No doubt the *that* was omitted in this line to bring the two *meets* closer and hence to enhance the wit found in the line. After verbs of command and entreaty the subjunctive is also found, as in:

I pray, his absence
Proceed by swallowing that (*Cym.* III v 58–9)

and

Thy Dukedome I resigne, and doe entreat
Thou pardon me my wrongs. (*Temp.* V i 118–19)

Such examples are not, however, likely to cause much problem to the average student.

The variation between subjunctive and indicative forms may sometimes be introduced for euphony or metrical necessity. Furthermore, it always remains possible that the compositors of the quartos or folios altered some of the endings to bring them into line with their own practice. Nevertheless, a student should always try to look for the difference between the subjunctive and the indicative, for this may be significant in highlighting the portrayal of character or the tone of a particular scene. Thus in *King Richard the Third* the Duchess of York can say to Richard:

My Prayers on the aduerse party fight,
And there the little soules of *Edwards* Children,
Whisper the Spirits of thine Enemies,
And promise them Successe and Victory:
Bloody thou art, bloody will be thy end:
Shame serues thy life, and doth thy death attend. (IV iv 190–5)

In this passage *fight, whisper* and *promise* are in the subjunctive, which expresses the duchess's wishes as to what may happen to Richard. The wish underlines her own powerlessness against Richard. However, the indicative of the final verbs underlines her conviction, which is here shown to be a certainty through that verbal mood, that Richard is indeed going to come to an ignoble end; the *doth* indicates almost a formal curse. Her powerlessness to act herself is matched by the certainty that she will be revenged in the end through Richard's miserable death.

The interchange between subjunctive and infinitive may at times add to the meaning as well as the euphony of a passage, as is the case in one of the most evocative uses of the subjunctive in Shakespeare:

> If it were done, when 'tis done, then 'twer well,
> It were done quickly. (*Macb.* I vii 1–2)

It would clearly be too heavy to have four subjunctive forms of *were* within the compass of fourteen words; the introduction of *is* gives variety to the sound and rhythm of the passage. It also gives added meaning to what Macbeth is saying. The subjunctive might have been anticipated since the proposition is apparently hypothetical. The use of the subjunctive in only some of the clauses implies that it is only the timing and the method of the killing which are in doubt; the assassination itself is evidently now for him a fact. The subsequent monologue represents his attempt to come to terms with this fact.

The model verbs such as *can, may* and *might* existed originally in English as full verbs, that is they occurred in a verbal group as the verb element. During the end of the Middle Ages and during the early Elizabethan period they developed their role as modals, though by Shakespeare's time they had not entirely lost their original characteristics, which have since been lost to the language. Hence examples occur in Shakespeare where what is the modern auxiliary is the main verb with both subject and object. In *The Tempest can* occurs in the sense 'knows' in 'the strongst suggestion, Our worser Genius can' (IV i 26–7). In this example many modern readers might be tempted to understand *can* as a modal with the main verb left unexpressed. *Will* occurs in the sense 'wish for' in 'I stand aloofe, and will no reconcilement' (*Ham.* V ii 239). In both cases the verb has both subject and object. However, these uses are not common in Shakespeare, for these verbs had largely developed modal roles.

Can, *may* and *might* need to be considered together since their meanings overlap. *Can* occurs much more frequently than *may*, and it is particularly frequent with a personal subject perhaps because of its original meaning 'know how to'. It is possible that *can*, at least in the negative, was considered more emphatic than *may* as the following passage from *The Taming of the Shrew* suggests:

TRA.: Let vs intreat you stay till after dinner.
PET.: It may not be.
GRA.: Let me intreat you.
PET.: It cannot be. (III ii 194–6)

As can be seen from this example both auxiliaries can have the sense of 'must', though this function is more commonly supplied by *may* than *can* which possibly accounts for the latter's emphasis in the passage quoted. *Can*, on the other hand, either means 'to be able to' as in Modern English or takes on the meaning of modern *may* as in 'Here can I sit alone, vn-seene of any' (*TGV* V iv 4).

May has a much wider meaning than its modern counterpart, for it covers the range of permission as well as the sense of 'can, be able to'. The latter is clear in Bassanio's 'May you sted me?' (*Merch.* I iii 7), which has the sense 'Can you provide me with the money?' There is no sense of permission involved. *Might* acts as the preterite form of *may* and has the same range of meaning. Consequently it frequently has the sense 'could' as in:

Heralds, from off our towres we might behold
From first to last, the on-set and retyre
Of both your Armies . . . . (*John* II i 325–7)

Although *might* more usually expresses the preterite, it can answer to the present and in some instances corresponds directly to *can*.

ANG.: Looke what I will not, that I cannot doe.
ISAB.: But might you doe't & do the world no wrong.
(*Meas.* II ii 52–3)

Here *might* means no more than 'you can do it'. The greater range of *may* and *might* in Shakespearian English is indicated by their use in interrogative sentences whereas in Modern English they are largely confined to declarative ones. The following question in *King Henry the Fifth* would not in Modern English be expressed with *may*:

> May it be possible, that forraigne hyer
> Could out of thee extract one sparke of euill
> That might annoy my finger? (II ii 100–2)

The use of *may* to express 'must' has already been noted. At the other end of the scale its inclusion is almost redundant or at best suggests a kind of weak possibility. When Silence says 'a score of good Ewes may be worth tenne pounds' (*2H4* III ii 50), he means that they are possibly worth ten pounds. In other instances it suggests what should be obvious to all, as in:

> If you may please to thinke I loue the King,
> And through him, what's neerest to him. (*WT* IV iv 513–14)

Since Camillo the speaker has been the servant of the king and his son for a long time, he is here expressing through *may* a self-evident truth.

May and *might*, particularly the latter, express the idea of wish and so correspond to Modern English 'I would like, be disposed to'. This sense may readily be misinterpreted by modern readers. In *The Two Gentlemen of Verona* the following exchange takes place:

> 3 OUT.: Haue you long soiourn'd there?
> VAL.: Some sixteene moneths, and longer might haue staid,
> If crooked fortune had not thwarted me. (IV i 20–2)

Here it is tempting to understand *might* in the more modern sense of 'would have been able' instead of in the Elizabethan meaning of 'would have liked'. When Horatio has seen the ghost for the first time in *Hamlet*, he exclaims:

> Before my God, I might not this beleeue
> Without the sensible and true auouch
> Of mine owne eyes (I i 56–8)

where *might* has the sense 'I would not like to believe, I would not be disposed to believe' rather than the simple 'I could not believe this'.

Must as today expresses necessity. It does, however, have a more generalised sense of what is going to happen or what is destined to happen. When Lorenzo says to Jessica 'Descend, for you must be my torch-bearer' (*Merch.* II vi 40), he does not so much imply necessity as futurity. The sense is 'You are going to be' or 'You will be'. This meaning is equally apparent in *Troilus and Cressida* when Thersites says of Ajax 'Hee must fight singly to morrow with *Hector*' (III iii 247). At the end of *Macbeth* when Macbeth says to Macduff:

> I beare a charmed Life, which must not yeeld
> To one of woman borne (V viii 12–13)

his use of *must not* seems to imply 'is not destined to'. If necessity is involved, it is a supernatural one.

The case of *shall* and *will* is a little more complicated if only because many readers bring to older texts their memories of the grammatical division of futurity between these two. Originally *shall* implied obligation or necessity, whereas *will* indicated volition. Both these could easily shade off into the sense of futurity, and as English originally had no separate future tense these two came to express it as they developed into auxiliaries. Because of their original meanings it was suggested by later grammarians that *shall* implied futurity only in the first person and *will* in the second and third. However true this may be for later periods of English, it does not apply to Elizabethan English where both can be used indiscriminately to express futurity. It is not necessary to illustrate this meaning with quotation. It may naturally be difficult on occasion to decide whether futurity alone is meant or whether a sense of destiny or necessity is also involved. In the last paragraph we saw that *must* had the meaning 'is going to be'. *Shall* is closely related in meaning to *must* and sometimes shares this same sense. In an earlier passage which corresponds to the quotation from *The Merchant of Venice* quoted in the last paragraph, we find Lorenzo saying 'Faire *Iessica* shall be my Torch-bearer' (II iv 39). In this instance *shall* has the same meaning of *must* which is something like 'is going to be'. The sense of definite futurity which shades off into obligation is still strong for *shall.* When Solanio in *The Merchant of Venice* says:

> Let good *Anthonio* looke he keepe his day
> Or he shall pay for this (II viii 25–6)

he means that he will certainly have to pay the penalty. This particular meaning of *shall*, which is not shared by *will*, is brought out in this quotation from *King Henry the Fifth*:

> Nay, it will please him well, *Kate*; it shall please him
> (V ii 245)

where the *shall* indicates a certainty not expressed through *will*. *Shall* can also be used in the modal sense of 'may'. When Hamlet dismisses his friends after the first appearance of the ghost, he says:

> I hold it fit that we shake hands, and part:
> You, as your busines and desires shall point you . . . .
> (*Ham.* I v 128–9)

The meaning here seems to be no more than 'may', though there may be the implication of 'ought to' since he adds 'For euery man ha's businesse and desire'. In *Julius Caesar* when Brutus says:

> What *Antony* shall speake, I will protest
> He speakes by leaue, and by permission (III i 239–40)

he certainly means 'Whatever Antony may say'. With verbs of seeing, thinking and finding, *shall* was commonly found in the sense of 'may' or 'will'. The implication is often that of the certainty of a self-evident truth. The sense of 'may' also occurs in subordinate clauses of purpose. When Iago says in *Othello*:

> that you shal surely find him
> Lead to the Sagitary the raised Search (I i 158–9)

he means 'In order that you may find him without fail'.

Will originally implied intention and it is difficult to separate futurity from intention in many examples of *will* in Shakespeare. Volition is clear in such examples as 'All Soules that will be safe, flye from my side' (*R2* III ii 80), just as futurity is unambiguous in 'the Duke himselfe will be to morrow at Court' (*MWW* IV iii 2). In between there are examples which may be taken either way, though one should always be aware of the possibility of intention in *will*. When in *King Richard the Second* York says:

It may be I will go with you: but yet Ile pawse,
For I am loth to breake our Countries Lawes (II iii 168–9)

both examples of *will* indicate some volition, though the former comes nearer to a simple future. *Will* often is used where a simple present might be expected and here one may assume that there is perhaps a stylistic effect indicating a more formal level of discourse. Thus Menenius in *Coriolanus* says 'I will be bold to take my leaue of you' (II i 89) immediately before departing, and in this his speech is echoed by others. In other instances the *will* may indicate emphasis rather after the manner of *do*, as we saw earlier. This certainly seems to be the case in the frequent use of expressions like *I'll tell you* and *I'll be sworn*. In yet other instances *will* indicates what is customary where again in Modern English *do* would be the more regular usage. The doctor in *Macbeth* enunciates a universal truth when he says:

infected mindes
To their deafe pillowes will discharge their Secrets. (V i 70–1)

An even more emphatic use of *will* occurs in:

'Tis so strange,
That though the truth of it stands off as grosse
As blacke and white, my eye will scarsely see it. (*H5* II ii 102–4)

In this case *will* means rather more perhaps than just 'does'. It approximates more closely to something like 'would not under any circumstances'.

Should and *would* are the original preterites of *shall* and *will*. As preterites they are not felt to be so forceful or imperative as the present tense forms and so they come to be used for the expression of condition as well as of unfulfilled wishes. The two were not kept apart and in many instances they appear to be used interchangeably, often indeed taking on the meaning 'could' as well. In 'But thou should'st please me better, would'st thou weepe' (*R2* III iv 20), there is little difference between the two, though *would'st* may imply 'if you are willing to'. Certainly *should* has the sense of 'can, could' in examples like 'where the diuell should hee learne our language?' (*Temp.* II ii 63), i.e. where can he possibly have learned our language?, and 'Where shold this Musick be?' (*Temp.* I ii 387), i.e. where can this music come from? Because of the sense of obligation in *shall*, *should* developed the meaning 'ought to be', though this can frequently be an emphatic form of 'is'. When Othello exclaims 'By Heauen, that should be my Handkerchiefe' (*Oth.* IV i 155), he uses *should* for emphasis, though he may also imply that he is not yet certain that the handkerchief is his. A more straightforward example where the sense of 'ought' is unambiguous is:

> I should report that which I say I saw,
> But know not how to doo't. (*Macb.* V v 31–2)

From this meaning of *should*, *should have* acquired the sense of 'was going to, ought to have' as in 'his Sonne, that should haue marryed a Shepheards Daughter' (*WT* IV iv 755). *Should* frequently occurs in the expression *as who should say*, meaning 'as if someone might say'. In some cases *should* seems inexplicable as when Rosalind asks Celia in *As You Like It* 'But didst thou heare without wondering, how thy name should be hang'd and carued vpon these trees?' (III ii 160–1). In interrogatives *should* has an emphatic implication which adds a sense of surprise to the question as in 'What should be in that *Cæsar*? Why should that name be sounded more then yours?' (*JC* I ii 142–3). *Would* implies a wish, but it seems not to have been as emphatic as *will* to judge from the following example from *Othello*, where *will* has a much stronger sense of intention:

> IAGO: I do repent me, that I put it to you.
> You would be satisfied?
> OTH.: Would? Nay, and I will. (III iii 396–7)

Would also indicates a past wish as in 'I would I had ore-look'd the Letter' (*TGV* I ii 50). Although this sense of wishing or volition is often present in *would*, it cannot be assumed that it is a regular feature of the word which, as we have seen, in many cases is indistinguishable from *should.*

The auxiliaries had developed by Elizabethan times, but they were not used as much as in Modern English and had not developed such a complicated variety of forms. The verbs in Shakespeare are thus rather simpler and more powerful than their modern counterparts. This is in part attributable also to the wide use of functional shift found in his writings, for by this means some of the semantic weight associated with nouns was transferred to the verbs. Antony's 'Would'st thou be window'd in great Rome' (*Ant.* IV xiv 72) shows this effect convincingly; and other examples are not hard to find. The simplicity of the verbs comes from the few tenses that were used, for there was a reliance on the simple forms of the present and preterite. The present occurs frequently because it gives immediacy to the description and force to the action. Although some examples of the use of the present might fall under the heading of the historic present, Shakespeare's uses of the present tense are far wider than such a title implies. When Douglas says 'That's the worst Tidings that I heare of yet' (*1H4* IV i 127), the present tense seems to reinforce the superlative because of its immediacy. The simple preterite can also be used where we today would employ the past tense, which usually implies that the action in the past is still operative at the time when the utterance is made. Belarius can say when he sees Cloten in *Cymbeline*:

> I saw him not these many yeares, and yet
> I know 'tis he (IV ii 67–8)

where we would have said 'I have not seen him'.

Another aspect of Shakespeare's verbal forms is the number of transitive verbs which occur without the extension which would be found in Modern English. Shakespeare could write 'ere we could arriue the Point propos'd' (*JC* I ii 110), which today would be 'arrive at'. The omission of this part of the verbal group also helps to give Shakespeare's verbs greater simplicity, and this verbal type is found in some of his memorable lines. Kent's 'Smoile you my speeches' (*Lear* II ii 77) is one of the better known examples.

The passive was formed by a part of the verb 'to be' or 'to have' with the past participle. Today the latter is the regular form, for it implies the activity needed to cause the state in question. The verb 'to be' merely expresses a state, as distinct from the activity, and so we distinguish between 'the tree is fallen' and 'the tree has fallen'. We think of the latter as the passive, for the former seems to be no different in structure from such statements as 'the tree is green', for both describe a state of the tree. In Shakespeare the verb 'to be' is used usually with verbs of motion as in 'I am arriu'd for fruitfull *Lumbardie*' (*Shrew* I i 3). Sometimes it is not very clear whether a state or the activity is implied. When Thurio says 'How now, sir *Protheus*, are you crept before vs?' (*TGV* IV ii 18), he may mean either, though the activity is more probable. The same ambiguity is found in Leontes's 'Was hee met there?' (*WT* II i 33). When Macbeth says:

> I am in blood
> Stept in so farre, that should I wade no more,
> Returning were as tedious as go ore (III iv 136–8)

he means that he has stepped into blood so far and not that he is steeped in it. The latter sense may be more appealing to many modern readers because of the *am* and *in*. The use of the verb 'to be' in passive constructions also makes it difficult to decide whether it is better to interpret what seem like identical structures in different ways. With '*Clarence* is well spoken' (*R3* I iii 348) the past participle would be interpreted as an adjective. But in 'Poor knaue, thou art ore-watch'd' (*JC* IV iii 239) there might be reason to assume that we have here a passive form, though elsewhere *ore-watch'd* is used in the phrase 'weary and o're-watch'd' (*Lear* II ii 165) where it is clearly adjectival. The boundary between the passive and the verb 'to be' with an adjective is impossible to delimit, and this may affect how much activity one reads into certain lines. Where a verb has an extension in Shakespeare, it is possible for that verb to have a passive form so that the subject of the verb is also the object of the preposition which forms the extension. In *Romeo and Juliet* a succession of such verbs occurs in 'You are lookt for, and cal'd for, askt for, & sought for' (I v 9–10). A more complicated example is 'he may be more wondred at' (*1H4* I ii 194), though its meaning is not likely to cause any difficulty.

Two verb forms which are much commoner in Shakespeare's language than today are the reflexive and the impersonal. The former may be attributable to the preponderance of transitive verb forms so that *I do repent me* (*R2* V iii 52) seems preferable to *I repent.* Some like *I feare me* (*2H6* I i 145) may be misunderstood, though the sense is simply 'I am afraid'. Impersonal verbs are those which have *it* or some other impersonal word as subject, though in Shakespeare that subject is often omitted. When Polonius says 'Well be with you Gentlemen' (*Ham.* II ii 376), we must assume an *it* as the subject of *be.* Many impersonal verbs originally had the apparent object in the dative form so that 'it pleases you' implied 'it pleases to you'. As impersonal verbs became less common this apparent object has become the subject. Thus *methinks* is now *I think.* In some instances in

Shakespeare it is not possible to tell whether a word is the subject or object. When in *King Richard the Third* the pursuivant says 'The better, that your Lordship please to aske' (III ii 99), it is possible to take *your Lordship* as the subject or object. In fact the quartos here read 'it please your Lordship', which makes the impersonal verb quite clear. Where the *it* follows the verb it may not always be possible to decide whether it is subject or not. When Hamlet says of the dead Polonius 'but heauen hath pleas'd it so, To punish me with this' (*Ham.* III iv 173–4), it may mean 'heaven decreed it' or 'it pleased heaven to arrange it'. The difference is one more of emphasis.

The infinitive in Elizabethan English has a wider range of meaning than today. It appears indiscriminately with or without *to*. This variety can appear strange to modern readers when the same main verb has an extension both with and without *to*, as in:

> Whether hadst thou rather be a *Faulconbridge*,
> And like thy brother to enioy thy land . . . . (*John* I i 134–5)

Here *be* and *to enioy* depend upon *hadst*. In Modern English the *to* can be omitted, but the circumstances under which that happens are regulated, whereas in Shakespeare's writings the presence or absence of the *to* was probably dictated by metrical and rhythmical considerations. The absence of *to* can naturally lead to syntactic ambiguity. In *Love's Labour's Lost* there is an example which shows the infinitive to be parallel to the participle:

> To see great *Hercules* whipping a Gigge,
> And profound *Salomon* tuning a Iygge?
> And *Nestor* play at push-pin with the boyes,
> And *Critticke Tymon* laugh at idle toyes. (IV iii 163–6)

Here, *whipping*, *tuning*, *play* and *laugh* all occupy the same syntactic position. When in *King Henry the Fifth* Exeter says to the French king 'Willing you ouer-looke this Pedigree' (II iv 90), it is possible that *ouer-looke* is a subjunctive meaning 'that you should look over'. It can, however, be understood as an infinitive without *to*. After verbs of command and request, it is possible to interpret the following verb as infinitive or imperative when there is no *to*. When Regan says to Oswald 'pray you giue him this' (*Lear* IV v 33) the *giue* can be interpreted as a command, which might then necessitate a comma after *you*, or as an infinitive dependent upon the *pray*. When a few lines later Regan says 'I pray desire her call her wisedome to her', the *call* may more readily be understood as an infinitive, though *desire* could be either. In *Othello* when Emilia says 'My Husband say she was false?' (V ii 155) *say* is probably an infinitive, though it may be understood as interrogative. This use of the infinitive with its own subject used to complete an utterance is paralleled in 'All Sects, all Ages smack of this vice, and he To die for't' (*Meas.* II ii 5–6). When the Duchess of Gloucester says to Gaunt 'In that thou seest thy wretched brother die' (*R2* I ii 27) the *dye* is an infinitive after a nominal group which together form the object of *seest*.

We are accustomed today to the use of the infinitive as either subject or object of a sentence, though it is a construction which appears to be much less common than it was. In Elizabethan English it was equally possible to have a noun and an infinitive in such a position, though we now would have a subordinate clause instead. When Leontes says:

> I haue deseru'd
> All tongues to talke their bittrest (*WT* III ii 212–13)

he means 'that all tongues should talk'. This usage is made clearer in this passage from *The Second Part of King Henry the Fourth* where the noun and infinitive are paralleled by a subordinate clause:

> which to proue fruite,
> Hope giues not so much warrant, as Dispaire
> That Frosts will bite them. (I iii 39–41)

Here, *to proue fruite* in the first clause has the same syntactic role as *That Frosts will bite them* in the second. Examples of this construction are unfamiliar to modern readers, and may be misunderstood.

Another use of the infinitive which can be misunderstood results from the confusion between it and the participles. The infinitive usually denoted purpose in pre-Shakespearian English, but Shakespeare's attempt to pack a lot of meaning into his utterances may have led to its being employed in other meanings. Since these other meanings are not found in Modern English, it is easy to assume that purpose is implied in the Shakespearian passage. When the messenger in *Macbeth* says to Lady Macduff 'To fright you thus. Me thinkes I am too sauage' (IV ii 69), he does not mean 'in order to frighten you', but 'by frightening you in this way'. The punctuation in the Folio may suggest the compositor was puzzled by the sense intended. A similar example occurs in *The Winter's Tale* where the gaoler says 'I know not what I shall incurre, to passe it' (II ii 57), where the sense is 'by allowing it to go, if I allow it to go'. By this means Shakespeare is able to achieve an elliptical style pregnant with meaning, though the syntax can too easily be misinterpreted today.

The infinitive can be used in a passive sense, though other meanings can also be involved. When Sebastian in *Twelfth Night* says 'What's to do? (III iii 18), he can mean 'What is there to be done?' or 'What is going on?' or even 'What is worth doing?'. Certainly in *Antony and Cleopatra* when Caesar says 'That's the next to do' (II vi 59), he means 'that's the next thing to be done'. But in *The Comedy of Errors* the infinitive would be understood more as an adjective when Angelo says 'And I too blame haue held him heere too long' (IV i 47), for the *too blame* is best taken as an infinitive meaning 'worthy to be blamed'.

Some aspects of the participles have already been dealt with in the previous chapter. Some examples are difficult to explain. When Buckingham says:

> Because, my Lord, I would haue had you heard
> The Traytor speake (*R3* III v 56–7)

it is not clear how *heard* is best interpreted grammatically. It may be an elliptical form of the past infinitive standing for 'to have heard' or it may be a past participle standing in some kind of loose relation to *you*. Similarly in *The Winter's Tale* the phrase 'The partie try'd' (III ii 2) is best interpreted as 'the defendant to be judged'. Shakespeare uses the participles to achieve compression, and their exact meaning and grammatical role are sometimes far from certain.

The participles had developed a variety of meanings during the development of English partly through the confusion of morphological endings and partly through the syntactic flexibility of the earlier language. Thus *beholding* seems to have been confused with *beholden* through the slurred pronunciation of the final unstressed syllable, and this may have allowed many participles in *-ing* to adopt a more active sense. Furthermore, the sense is often different from the one that might be expected in Modern English. When Cressida says:

> Women are Angels wooing,
> Things won are done (*Troil.* I ii 278–9)

it would be understandable to take the *wooing* as a qualifier to *women* which fulfils the same function as *won* to *Things*. The sentence does not mean 'when women are wooing', but rather 'when women are being wooed'. The *wooing* acts as a clause on its own, as though the rest of its clause had been omitted. This is a frequent construction in Shakespeare in which the participle can stand in a variety of syntactic relations to the main verb, for there is no conjunction to express what that relationship should be. Condition and causality are readily implied through this construction. This can be seen through parallel clauses as in *All's Well that Ends Well*:

> not helping, death's my fee,
> But if I helpe, what doe you promise me. (II i 188–9)

Here the parallelism of the clauses shows that *not helping* means 'If I do not help'. A more complicated example is found in *The Winter's Tale*:

> though I with Death, and with
> Reward, did threaten and encourage him,
> Not doing it, and being done. (III ii 160–2)

Here the final line means 'If he did not do it, and if it was done', and each clause refers respectively to the *threaten* and *encourage* of the previous line. Camillo was threatened if he did not do it and encouraged to do it. Causality is expressed through the participle when Regan says 'being his Knaue, I will' (*Lear* II ii 132) which means 'because you are his servant, I will (do it)'. In all these instances the participles have a quasi-verbal function for the nouns to which they might be subordinate are not included, and so they achieve an absolute status. It may be that this structure was developed partly through the influence of the Latin ablative absolute.

Similar compression occurs with the past participle. When Cominius says:

> where Ladies shall be frighted,
> And gladly quak'd, heare more (*Cor.* I ix 5–6)

the *gladly quak'd* appears to mean 'where ladies have been made to tremble in a way that brought them entertainment'. In *The Comedy of Errors* the sense of:

> Sweet recreation barr'd, what doth ensue
> But moodie and dull melancholly (V i 78–9)

is 'If pleasurable recreation is prevented, . . .'. It is probably the use of such participial constructions which encouraged Shakespeare to use other adjectives in a similar environment. Bolingbroke in *King Richard the Second* can say 'Ioy absent, greefe is present for that time' (I iii 259), which presumably means 'If joy is absent', though it could be readily imply 'While joy is absent' or something similar. This use of the participles and associated words enabled Shakespeare to write a very elliptical language, which it is sometimes difficult to interpret. This is an aspect of the relationship between the various clauses in an utterance – a matter to which I shall return.

6 Adverbs, Prepositions and Conjunctions

In the last chapter little was said of extensions because these are not so likely to cause difficulty to modern readers and because they are often formed of prepositions which could be alternatively interpreted as adverbs. This applies also in Modern English since the extension may be separated from the verb element of the verbal group. Hence we can say 'Drink up your beer' or 'Drink your beer up'. The unfamiliarity of Shakespearian idiom may sometimes make it difficult to decide whether a word like *up* should be interpreted as part of the verbal group or as an independent adverb, although the difference in meaning is not likely to be great. When Shakespeare writes 'To fill the mouth of deepe Defiance vp' (*1H4* III ii 116), it is possible to take *vp* either way, and most readers would probably think of it as the extension in the verbal group *fill vp*. Shakespeare has separated the *vp* from the verb to throw it into emphasis and so it has more the function of an adverb with the sense 'to the brim, completely'. It is perhaps better to think of it as an adverb in order to bring home this extra meaning which Shakespeare intended. A more tricky example is provided in *King Richard the Third* when Richard says:

for it stands me much vpon
To stop all hopes, whose growth may dammage me. (IV ii 60–1)

Here *vpon* is to be taken as the extension of the verb with the sense 'is incumbent upon, is imperative for', rather than as a preposition which has been placed after the noun or pronoun it governs. However, in *Hamlet* the order of *stand* and *vpon* is reversed in:

the moist starre,
Vpon whose influence *Neptunes* Empier stands . . . . (I i 118–19, Q2)

Here *stands vpon* could be taken as a verbal group meaning 'is dependent on', though the word order may encourage readers to think that *vpon* has here more the nature of a preposition. However, extensions in verbal groups are not met with so frequently in Shakespeare because it was more usual to use prefixes to the verb. One might expect to find Elizabethan English preferring to use a verb form like *to outtake* rather than one like *to take out*. It was the gradual fall in the use of living prefixes which has caused the explosion of verbal extensions in Modern English. This meant that the relation between adverbial forms and extension of the verbal phrase was still unclear as in the case of *stand vpon*. Other examples are not hard to find. They all show that there was a close relationship between adverb and preposition. In addition, the relation between conjunction and either adverb or preposition is close, and this is why this chapter is concerned with all three.

The adverb has many different origins, and there are few parts of speech that have not been converted into adverbs. In Old English adverbs were most commonly formed from adjectives through the addition of the ending *-a*. With the weak stress position it occupied at the end of the word, this *-a* was reduced at first to *-e* and then finally disappeared so that there was no difference in form between an adjective and an adverb. This situation upset the eighteenth-century grammarians who recommended that adverbs should end in *-ly* with the result that this ending was accepted as a sign of the adverb. Many adverbs without it were lost and most new ones since then tend to have it. This situation, however, did not prevail in Shakespearian times so that it is often impossible to tell whether an adjective or an adverb is intended. It may well be that Shakespeare himself did not know, for often it makes little difference to the sense whichever grammatical interpretation is made. When Polixenes says:

> We were (faire Queene)
> Two Lads, that thought there was no more behind,
> But such a day to morrow, as to day,
> And to be Boy eternall (*WT* I ii 62–5)

the final word can be understood as an adjective following the noun or as an adverb dependent upon *be*. The latter seems more likely, though the form of *eternall* may encourage modern readers to favour the former. The situation of these forms is confused by the occurrence of adjectives with the *-ly* ending, as is still true of one or two words today like *lovely*. When a form with *-ly* and one without occur in the same phrase, the difficulty of deciding whether one is dealing with adjectives or adverbs is compounded. In *King Richard the Second* we find the sentence:

> The Duke of Norfolke, sprightfully and bold,
> Stayes but the summons of the Appealants Trumpet. (I iii 3–4)

Here *sprightfully* might well be an adverb, particularly as *sprightful* occurs elsewhere in Shakespeare. *Bold*, on the other hand, suggests an adjectival form. It would in fact be possible to interpret this phrase as a qualifier to *Duke of Norfolke* or as an adverbial group looking forward to *Stayes*. Sometimes there may be quite a sharp difference in emphasis depending on which interpretation is used. When Polonius says to Ophelia:

> I doe know
> When the Bloud burnes, how Prodigall the Soule
> Giues the tongue vowes (*Ham.* I iii 115–17)

prodigall can be interpreted as an adverb or an adjective. It may be any soul which gives prodigally or only the prodigal soul which gives. *All* is a frequent source of confusion. In some instances it seems clearly to be an adverb as in:

> I will choose
> Mine heyre from forth the Beggers of the world,
> And dispossesse her all. (*Tim.* I i 140–2)

The sense 'entirely' is appropriate here. In *The Winter's Tale* it is interpreted as an adjective in:

> Your Honors all,
> I doe referre me to the Oracle (III ii 112–13)

an interpretation supported by the punctuation in the Folio. But *all* could mean 'entirely, absolutely' here too and such a reading would reinforce the emphasis found in the verbal form *I doe referre*.

Today the adverbial group can occur in a variety of positions in the sentence, though in Elizabethan times this freedom of positioning was even greater. This freedom itself adds to the ambiguities of interpretation. In the following passage:

> The silence often of pure innocence
> Perswades, when speaking failes (*WT* II ii 41–2)

often is usually regarded as an adverb qualifying *perswades*. This makes the statement somewhat weak, as silence will only conquer from time to time. Yet *often* is inserted in the middle of a nominal group, which is an unusual place to locate an adverb. Shakespeare does use *often* (and *oft*) as a modifier with the sense 'frequent, continual'. When Jacques says 'my [*Folio* by] often rumination, wraps me in a most humorous sadnesse' (*AYL* IV i 17–18), modern scholars do not interpret *often* as an adverb, though it could be so interpreted with as much propriety as the example from *The Winter's Tale.* We have already seen how common it is in Shakespeare to have an adjective in the qualifier slot, and so there would seem no reason to deny that *often* should in *The Winter's Tale* be taken as an adjective. This would then make the sentence mean 'The continual silence of pure innocence persuades . . . ', a statement which is much more vigorous and more appropriate for Paulina than the one normally attributed to her. It stresses her confidence and determination.

Another example of potential ambiguity occurs later in the same play. When Antigonus deposits the baby Perdita in Bohemia, he says:

> there these,
> Which may if Fortune please, both breed thee (pretty)
> And still rest thine. (III iii 47–9)

The *these* refers to the jewels and money he lays beside her. These riches may assist her to be looked after and still remain in her possession. The problem in this passage resides in the *pretty*. Most interpreters understand it to be a noun and, following the brackets of the Folio, place it within commas, as though Antigonus were using it as a form of address, which would be parallel to *Blossome* a few lines earlier. The Arden editor glosses these lines 'both be enough to pay for your upbringing, pretty one, and still leave something for your future use'.[1] However, *pretty* could be interpreted as an adverb (or even an adjective for that matter) referring back to *breed*. To *breed pretty* would mean 'to bring up elegantly or in a courtly manner' and it would give more point to what Antigonus has to say. He does not mean that she will merely be looked after, but that the gold will ensure that she is brought up in a decent way, because the riches will suggest to the finder that the foundling is someone of substance. An interpretation of *pretty* as an adverb would, therefore, seem to give the statement greater force.

The freedom in the positioning of the adverb may lead to other kinds of ambiguity. In the same play the following lines occur:

> whose Loue had spoke,
> Euen since it could speake, from an Infant, freely,
> That it was yours. (III ii 67–9)

Here the two adverbs *from an Infant* and *freely* are found after the second clause. They may both refer to the second clause 'since it could readily speak from infancy' or to the first clause 'whose love had readily proclaimed from childhood', or they may be divided in reference to both the preceding clauses 'whose love had readily proclaimed from the very moment it could speak in childhood'. Any of these interpretations seems acceptable, and it is not easy to decide which was intended.

There are many intensive adverbs in Shakespeare and, as we noted in the Introduction, intensives are among the more fleeting features of language. As vogue words they come and go quickly. It is not clear how far the many intensives Shakespeare used were common or how far they represent the striving after a linguistic effect. Many of them occur before an adjective and may seem strange or extravagant to modern readers. Those which occur more commonly may often be interpreted as part of a compound. Thus *all* may appear with or without a hyphen linking it to the following adjective. Generally *all humbled* as in 'And presently, all humbled kisse the Rod' (*TGV* I ii 59) occurs as two words, whereas *all-disgraced* as in 'her all-disgraced Friend' (*Ant.* III xii 22) occurs as one. Only a few instances of *all* as intensifier are likely to cause more than a momentary hesitation, as may be true of 'When all aloud the winde doth blow' (*LLL* V ii 908). Other intensifiers are certainly more unusual and may not be immediately understood as such, as is the case with *far* in:

I am a subiect fit to be ieast withall,
But farre vnfit to be a Soueraigne. (*3H6* III ii 91–2)

The range of intensives is impressive and includes *clean, clearly, great, marvellous*, *passing*, *shrewdly* and *throughly*. Among the most unusual are *plaguy* and *vengeance*, both of which are used to intensify *proud*. The first occurs in *Troilus and Cressida* where Achilles is described as 'so plaguy proud' (II iii 172), and the latter in *Coriolanus* where Coriolanus is said to be 'vengeance prowd' (II ii 5). An intensive does not need to intensify an adjective, but may be used to intensify a verb. These are less commonly met with today and some words would not occur as intensives at all. When in *Coriolanus* Marcius exclaims as the Romans are beaten back:

backes red, and faces pale
With flight and agued feare, mend and charge home (I iv 37–8)

he uses *home* as an intensive with the meaning 'to the utmost, extremely'. It occurs not infrequently in Shakespeare in this sense.

Naturally many adverbs had different meanings and uses in Shakespearian English from those found today, and a typical example is *almost*. It approximated then to the sense of modern 'even', particularly when used for emphasis. It could also be used with negatives in senses which have now been taken over by 'hardly' and 'hardly ever'. The emphatic sense of *almost* could easily be misunderstood in an expression such as:

Would you imagine, or almost beleeue (*R3* III v 35)

where *almost* expresses disbelief, i.e. 'Could you possibly imagine'. With negatives *almost* may also appear very difficult to interpret because the *almost* does not necessarily occur in close proximity with the negative; indeed, it is not unusual for *almost* to follow it. When a London citizen says 'You cannot reason (almost) with a man' (*R3* II iii 39), it is easy for a modern reader to be confused by the *almost* particularly in those modern editions which like the Folio print *cannot* as a single word. Here, as elsewhere, the *almost not* means no more than 'hardly'.

Negatives also differ considerably from their modern counterparts. The double negative was still a living idiom and was employed for emphasis. A good example is provided by Celia when she says: 'but loue no man in good earnest, nor no further in sport neyther' (*AYL* I ii 24). The use of *nor* where modern English might prefer *or* or even *and* can lead to uncertainty as to the precise meaning. When Portia says 'it is not hard *Nerrissa*, that I cannot choose one, nor refuse none' (*Merch.* I ii 22–3), she means she cannot choose or refuse anyone. *Never* occurs in contexts where we might expect *ever*, though its precise meaning is not easy to deduce. When Hermia says:

> Neuer so wearie, neuer so in woe,
> Bedabbled with the dew, and torne with briars,
> I can no further crawle, no further goe (*MND* III ii 442–4)

the first line seems to mean something like 'So weary as I am and so afflicted with sorrow'. It is parallel with the clauses in the second line which contain no negatives. Occasionally *never so* has the sense of 'however', as in 'be he ne're so vile' (*H5* IV iii 62), though that does not seem appropriate in the quotation from *A Midsummer Night's Dream*. *Never* and *nothing* were used as emphatic negatives. In the following exchange between Albany and Goneril, the latter's use of *never* as emphatic injects a little more venom into what she has to say:

> ALB.: Now Gods that we adore,
> Whereof comes this?
> GON.: Neuer afflict your selfe to know more of it. (*Lear* I iv 290–1)

Similarly in the same play when Lear utters his famous line consisting only of *never's*, he is using it as the emphatic form of *no* and so is using extreme hyperbole through an emphatic negative and its repetition five times. The use of *nothing* where Modern English prefers *not* can occasionally be misunderstood in those cases where the word order is different from that today. When Valeria says 'they nothing doubt preuailing' (*Cor.* I iii 99), the use of *nothing* and the present participle make the sense obscure to many modern readers. It is no more than 'They do not doubt to prevail (over the enemy)'.

Adverbs which govern the clause as a whole rather than a word or phrase within it are among the vogue words in English which change frequently. Among those which were common in Shakespeare are *belike, happily* or *haply*, and *withal.* Because Shakespeare uses a wide range of adverbs, it is not always easy to decide whether his examples refer to the clause or to some part of it. When Hamlet says 'I'm sorry they offend you heartily' (*Ham.* I v 134), he may use *heartily* to mean 'I am very sorry' or alternatively to mean 'Indeed, I am sorry to offend you'. The Folio punctuation which is followed by most editors and the occurrence in the next line of *Yes faith, heartily* suggest the latter interpretation. These adverbs which today occur either at the beginning or the end of the clause may in Shakespeare's English occur in the middle, as is true of several examples of *haply/happily*.

Prepositions constitute the most problematic wordclass in many languages, because their use and meaning seem so arbitrary; and this is certainly true of Elizabethan English. We have already seen how difficult it is to decide whether words following a verb form part of the verbal group or are to be considered as prepositions. The ease with which verbs could take a variety of different prepositions inclines one in many instances to the latter interpretation. A word like *repent* could be followed by *at, for, in, of* or *over*, and these alternatives make it appear as though there was no fixed verbal group consisting of verb and extension and as though the meaning of the various prepositions was not far apart. In fact it is characteristic of prepositions at an earlier period of the language that they all had a much wider range of meanings than we are accustomed to today. There were in the Elizabethan period fewer prepositions in any case, so each had to serve a wider function; as we have increased the number of prepositions by employing phrases and present participles in this role, so we have been able to restrict the range of meaning that each one carries. A good example is *at*. It can be used instead of *in* particularly preceding the names of larger cities, as 'I told him that your father was at *Venice*, And that you look't for him this day in *Padua*' (*Shrew* IV iv 15–16). It could have the sense of 'of, from' especially in association with verbs like *have*, *take* and *get*. In this sense it usually occurs in the phrase *at his hands*, as for example 'Haue you receiu'd no promise of satisfaction at her hands?' (*MWW* II ii 190). It was also used to indicate value or worth, a use which occurs frequently in Shakespeare. Timon says:

> But I do prize it at my loue, before
> The reuerends Throat in Athens. (*Tim.* V i 179–80)

Aufidius can speak of 'At a few drops of Womens rhewme' (*Cor.* V vi 46), where *at* implies 'for the price of, at the value of'. The sense 'to' seems most appropriate in 'But I will delue one yard belowe their mines, And blowe them at the Moone' (*Ham.* III iv 208–9, Q[2]). *At* occurs after certain verbs which do not take an extension today, though whether we should regard it in these instances as preposition or extension is not easy to decide. Constance says 'I enuie at their libertie' (*John* III iv 73). *Chid* is followed directly by *at* in 'when you chidde at Sir Protheus' (*TGV* II i 65), though they are separated in 'Chid I, for that at frugal Natures frame?' (*Ado* IV i 128). In the latter instance the separation could readily cause uncertainty as to the passage's meaning, for *frugal Natures frame* might not be understood as the object of *chid at*. Finally, *at* occurs in differing contexts with a specialised meaning, though it is not possible to detail all of these. A typical example is:

> I am too high-borne to be proportied
> To be a secondary at controll (*John* V ii 79–80)

where *at* might most satisfactorily be understood to mean 'under'.

Some words can act as preposition, adverb or conjunction although this is less likely today because we have often introduced a new word in at least one of these functions. Thus in Elizabethan times *after* could be adverb, preposition or conjunction, but today the adverbial form is *afterwards* and although *after* can still occur as a conjunction it is less commonly met with than previously. A problem that can arise over interpretation occurs because not all prepositions, despite their name, are found before the word they govern. This may cause particular problems in deciding whether the form is an adverb or a preposition. When Lepidus says 'pray you hasten your Generals after' (*Ant.* II iv 1–2), it may be that *after* is a postponed preposition, although it could as readily be interpreted as an adverb. Today *after* as a preposition is restricted to space or time, but in Elizabethan times it was also used to express manner. Stephano can say: 'He's in his fit now; and doe's not talke after the wisest' (*Temp.* II ii 70), where *after the wisest* seems to mean 'in the manner of his most rational fashion'. *After* as an adverb is used of time, though in some examples its occurrence with nouns functionally shifted to verbs can lead to uncertainty for modern readers. When Bolingbroke says 'A while to worke, and after holliday' (*R2* III i 44), the *after holliday* looks to modern readers like a preposition and noun, whereas it is an adverb and verb. *After* as a conjunction is frequently followed by *that*, a common element in Elizabethan conjunctions, as in 'After that things are set in order here, Wee'le follow them' (*1H6* II ii 32–3). The prepositions are important words which can modify the sense of a clause and so need to be interpreted correctly. However, there are few general guidelines which can be laid down and so students must consult a good glossary. Unfortunately they are not the words which are likely to be glossed in an average modern edition of Shakespeare.

The position of the conjunctions was not very different from that of the prepositions. In earlier periods of English there were fewer of them and consequently they each carried a wider range of meaning. More recently we have extended the number of conjunctions. In addition, we have tended in writing to increase the amount of subordination within sentences, a development which demands a greater number of conjunctions. In Elizabethan times it was more usual to construct sentences on a basis of parallelism or contrast, and although the two halves of a sentence might have a conjunction it need not follow that it had the same function as a conjunction today. Indeed, many seem to have filled the role of adverbs. This can still be true today, though it has been discouraged in more formal writing at least. To begin a sentence with *and*, for example, would be considered infelicitous now because there would be nothing before the *and* to be linked in a co-ordination with what follows it.

And is an excellent word to indicate many of the features of conjunctions in Shakespeare's works. It has several meanings, whereas today conjunctions have become more specialised in their senses, and it can be used more in the nature of an adverb than a conjunction. As an adverb it has the sense of 'even' and is used primarily for emphasis, as in 'When that I was and a little tine boy' (*TN* V i 375). At the beginning of sentences it approximates more closely to 'indeed' in meaning, though again its use implies emphasis where today it might seem merely fussy. This is indicated in the following quotation from *King Richard the Third*:

QU.: How canst thou woo her?
RICH.: That I would learne of you,
As one being best acquainted with her humour.
QU.: And wilt thou learne of me? (IV iv 267–9)

Elizabeth's final sentence means 'Will you really be instructed by me?' for the *and* has more weight than we today would give it. It emphasises a question and can reinforce an answer, as in the following example.

> PAR.: after them, and take a more dilated farewell.
> ROSS.: And I will doe so. (*A W* II i 55–6)

Here Bertram Count of Rossillion means 'That's just what I intend to do', and the emphasis is provided by the *and*. Even in cases where *and* might be suspected to have a co-ordinating function, it is used by Shakespeare more for emphasis, for in similar constructions it may be omitted. Thus when Carlisle says:

> And shall the figure of Gods Maiestie,
> His Captaine, Steward, Deputie elect,
> Anoynted, Crown'd, planted many yeeres,
> Be iudg'd by subiect, and inferior breathe,
> And he himselfe not present? (*R2* IV i 125–9)

there are two examples of *and*. The first adds emphasis to the question which has the sense 'Shall this really happen?' The second which appears in the last line might seem to be a straightforward co-ordinating conjunction, though the two items linked by the *and* are not identical in structure. In Shakespeare's English the *and* as a linking device is not necessary here and so co-ordination is not a satisfactory interpretation. The *and* might be translated as 'even though', except that would not convey the emphasis which the *and* implies. The last line suggests a translation such as 'Without the king actually being present', for the *and* implies incredulity. Sometimes the *and* links two clauses or phrases, though they might make better sense without it. In such cases co-ordination is hardly at stake, and once again we may infer emphasis. When Caliban says 'Here comes a Spirit of his, and to torment me' (*Temp.* II ii 15), the *and* and the comma suggest co-ordination. To some extent this is right for the sentence means something more than simply 'Here comes a spirit to torment me'. It means something like 'Here comes a spirit who is surely going to torment me'. This use of an emphatic *and* is common and can readily be overlooked, although to do so may destroy some of the emotional charge which Shakespeare wishes to impart to situations.

In the above instances *and* might more appropriately be classed as an adverb. In other cases it seems to have more of a conjunction's function, though more of a subordinating than a co-ordinating one. When York says:

> *Aumerle* that was,
> But that is lost, for being *Richards* Friend.
> And Madam, you must call him *Rutland* now (*R2* V ii 41–3)

the *and* may imply a causal relationship between the two clauses: because he lost his former name, he must now be called by the other one. *And* might therefore mean something like 'And consequently', though it could also be interpreted in the emphatic manner outlined in the preceding paragraph. *And* as a subordinating conjunction means 'if', and the two words frequently combine in the conjunction *and if*. Often *and* in this sense appears as *an* in either Folio or quartos. An example of its use is Pandarus's 'And her haire were not somewhat darker then *Helens*, well go too, there were no more comparison betweene the Women' (*Troil.* I i 41–2). This sense of *and* may be influenced by its more customary emphatic use so that *and* can mean 'if' in a more positive way. When a citizen says in *King Richard the Third*:

> O full of danger is the Duke of Glouster,
> And the Queenes Sons, and Brothers, haught and proud;
> And were they to be rul'd, and not to rule,
> This sickly Land, might solace as before (II iii 27–30)

the *and* at the beginning of the third line means 'if'. However, from the context it seems to be rather stronger than simply 'if', and perhaps means more 'if only' or 'if indeed'.

Another feature of conjunctions at this time is that they were frequently linked with *that* so that we find such examples as *after that*, *but that*, *if that* and *when that* among others. Although this addition of *that* is not in itself likely to cause difficulties to a modern reader, in cases where there are two parallel subordinate clauses, the *that* may be detached from the primary conjunction and appear at the beginning of the second clause. Hence we can find examples like the following:

> When he had carried Rome, and that we look'd
> For no lesse Spoile, then Glory . . . . (*Cor.* V vi 43–4)

Here the conspirator's words are interrupted by Aufidius, but it is clear that both clauses are temporal ones with the sense 'When he had conquered Rome and when we expected spoils and glory'. Instead of having *when that* together, they have been separated with one at the head of each clause. One instance which is frequently misunderstood by modern readers is the opening of Macbeth's famous soliloquy:

> If th'Assassination
> Could trammell vp the Consequence, and catch
> With his surcease, Successe: that but this blow
> Might be the be all, and the end all. (I vii 2–5)

In this quotation the *that* in the middle of line four means 'if' and the clause is parallel with what goes before. In many examples the result can appear very strange to a modern reader, as in:

> Howsoere, 'tis strange,
> Or that the negligence may well be laugh'd at:
> Yet is it true Sir. (*Cymb.* I i 65–7)

In this example the *howsoere* is an unfamiliar conjunction and so the rest of the sentence may be difficult to disentangle. The sense is 'However odd it may be or however much the negligence may be scoffed at, yet the facts are correct'. The use of *that* in a second, parallel, subordinate clause in examples like this paved the way for its use in similar positions where the first clause was not introduced by a conjunction, but by inversion. Sonnet 39 concludes in the following way:

> Oh absence what a torment wouldst thou proue,
> Were it not thy soure leisure gaue sweet leaue,
> To entertaine the time with thoughts of loue,
> Which time and thoughts so sweetly dost deceiue.
> And that thou teachest how to make one twaine,
> By praising him here who doth hence remaine.

In this sonnet Shakespeare expresses the condition through inversion of *Were it* rather than through *if*, though he introduces the second conditional clause by *that* as though *if* had been used. The interepretation of this sextet is made more complicated by the introduction of the relative clause between the two conditional ones, with the result that the *And that* might at first be thought to be parallel to the relative clause.

Other conjunctions show the same range of meaning and use as *and*, though it is not possible to consider further examples here. It is important to realise how closely related the adverbs, prepositions and conjunctions were in Shakespearian English for otherwise many passages may be misunderstood or their tone and emphasis ignored. The function of these words is intimately linked with the whole question of word order and the relationship of clauses to one another; and that forms the subject of the next chapter.

7 Word Order and Sentence Types

An aspect of Shakespeare's language which strikes modern readers immediately is the apparent liberty which he takes with word order. Some examples have been noted already in discussing the nominal group. One example was not considered in that chapter, namely the frequency with which the modifier is placed before the determiner. This change can cause ambiguity and may lead to difficulties in interpreting the type of sentence involved, which is why it has been left until now for consideration. Examples where the determiner and modifier change position are common enough, such as 'Gentle my Lord' (*WT* II i 98). It may readily be appreciated that this word order allows the modifier to be interpreted as having a different function in the sentence. When Ferdinand says:

> Let me liue here euer,
> So rare a wondred Father, and a wise
> Makes this place Paradise. (*Temp*. IV i 122–4)

it is tempting despite the comma in the Folio to understand *so rare* with what goes before rather than with what follows because there is a modifier *wondred* following the determiner already. It is, however, customary to take *So rare* as a modifier. Equally when Leontes calls his son 'Most dear'st, my Collop' (*WT* I ii 137), most editors keep the Folio's comma or even turn it into a heavier stop such as an exclamation mark. Yet the phrase could be understood as if it were 'My most dear'st Collop', i.e. my beloved child, which is in many ways preferable since such an interpretation parallels 'sweet Villaine' in the preceding line. The punctuation of the Folio is not necessarily authentic. Another interesting example occurs earlier in the same scene of this play. When Leontes fails to persuade Polixenes to stay longer, he turns to his queen to enlist her aid in the attempt to change their visitor's mind. According to the Folio he says 'Tongue-ty'd our Queene? speake you' (*WT* I ii 27), and this reading is followed by modern editors. The import of the question is not very clear. Leontes cannot be asking his wife if she is tongue-tied; he must presumably be enquiring why she is tongue-tied. It might be preferable, however, to ignore the Folio's question-mark (for as we shall see the punctuation of the Folio does not always reflect that of the earlier quartos in those plays where quartos are extant) and to understand *tongue-ty'd* as a modifier before the determiner. By this reading *Tongue-ty'd our Queene* would then be a form of address and the *tongue-ty'd* would be put into a closer relationship with *speake.* The sense would then be something like 'Speak up, my tongue-tied queen', which produces a more rhetorical reading. However, the problems of punctuation and types of sentence must be left till later in this chapter.

The alterations of word order are more likely to affect the placing of subject, verb and object. This freedom is still taken for granted by poets, though today the most usual change is the placing of the object at the start of the sentence. When that is done, misunderstanding is less likely to arise. Shakespeare, however, alters the word order much more drastically than this so that ambiguity can easily result. This ambiguity arises because English is not an inflected language and hence word order is the principal means to distinguish subject from object. A typical case of ambiguity is found in the following passage:

> This Entertainment
> May a free face put on: deriue a Libertie
> From Heartinesse, from Bountie, fertile Bosome,
> And well become the Agent. (*WT* I ii 111–14)

Here the second nominal group comes between the auxiliary and the verb and so it is possible to interpret it as subject or object: a free face may put on this entertainment or this entertainment may put on a free face. Since the sense is acceptable either way, it is not possible to decide which is right. The ease with which word order was modified for rhetorical purposes and the freedom to omit certain parts of speech make the following line ambiguous as well. *Fertile bosome* may be the third nominal group dependent upon a *from*, though in its case the *from* is missing; or it could be parallel to *Libertie* and thus a second object to *deriue* so that there was the rhetorical balance of object – prepositional group: prepositional group – object. Since these words are metaphorical abstracts either reading makes reasonable sense, though the former is that preferred by most editors.

A less obvious example, which also links the use of *and* as an adverb as noted in the last chapter, occurs in *Hamlet*:

> Oh such a deed,
> As from the body of Contraction pluckes
> The very soule, and sweete Religion makes
> A rhapsidie of words. (*Ham.* III iv 45–8)

That *such a deed* is the subject seems likely from its parallelism with *such an Act* earlier in the speech. The most acceptable reading is that *and* is adverbial and *makes* has two objects; so the sense is 'Such a deed even turns sweet religion into no more than a play of words'. This sense has to be teased out of the passage, for it is not immediately accessible to a modern reader.

The placing of the object first in the clause is a common enough phenomenon today, but Shakespeare frequently extends the nominal group acting as object by including one or more qualifiers so that readers begin to think that the object is going to be the subject and it comes as a shock when the real subject is introduced. Thus we have:

> these Proclamations,
> So forcing faults vpon *Hermione*,
> I little like. (*WT* III i 15–17)

The longer the qualifier, the more unexpected it is to find that the first nominal group is not the subject. The placing of the object after the subject but before the verb is not infrequent, particularly when it is a pronoun, as in 'I might not this beleeue' (*Ham.* I i 56). This arrangement allows the clause, and often the line, to finish on a more powerful word, the verb, than would otherwise be the case.

The alterations in word order may appear fussy or overdone to many modern readers, though there is usually good reason for them. Emphasis was an important consideration, as it still is today. Alteration in the word order may also help to point out the parallelism, as when Falstaff says 'him keepe with, the rest banish' (*1H4* II iv 415). It also brings items which are related in meaning closer together as in 'By Richard that dead is' (*1H4* I iii 146), where *Richard* and *dead* are made more immediately associated. Similarly in Sonnet 48 the word *iewels* in the fifth line is immediately undercut by the following *trifles* in 'But thou, to whom my iewels trifles are'. Word order can also be used to achieve rhetorical arrangements in which the meaning may sometimes be difficult to disentangle, particularly for an audience in a theatre. Thus two subject - verb - object groups which should logically follow each other can be amalgamated so that the two subjects are followed by the two verbs and then by the two objects. This may happen even when the two clauses are contrasted rather than parallel and when the constituents of the clause are different from the hypothetical example just mentioned. Hence we find:

> though I with Death, and with
> Reward, did threaten and encourage him,
> Not doing it, and being done. (*WT* III ii 160–2)

Here both clauses share the same subject *I* and object *him*, but otherwise they each have contrasted elements. The sense is 'I threatened him with death if he did not do it, and I encouraged him with reward if he did do it'. The arrangement adopted by Shakespeare allows each pair of contrasted features to be placed side by side.

Punctuation is an important matter which concerns both the cohesion of clauses and the interpretation of what kind of clause an utterance is, though not much work has been done on Shakespearian punctuation. The attitude of editors towards it has been ambivalent. Although they have freely modernised Shakespearian spelling, they have tended to preserve the basic features of the Folio punctuation although they have emended whenever they think the sense demands it. Alterations to the punctuation are rarely recorded in the apparatus criticus of editions, for they are felt to be part of the accepted modernisation which many editors undertake. It is impossible for readers to read through the editorial punctuation to that in the Folio to see whether a different reading may have been possible. The punctuation in the quartos and Folio is not static, for there is a trend to make the punctuation heavier in later versions. This may be, as has been suggested, an attempt to introduce some standardisation into the punctuation.[1] However that may be, the very symbols that are found in the quartos and Folio, for example, do not necessarily have the meanings which we today give them. A question mark may be used, for instance, where we would have an exclamation mark or nothing at all. Modern editors usually normalise examples of this type of question mark, though they are not in agreement which question marks indicate exclamations. In a passage from the Folio like the following:

> No, in good earnest.
> How sometimes Nature will betray it's folly?
> It's tendernesse? and make it selfe a Pastime
> To harder bosomes? (*WT* I ii 150–3)

most modern editors, but by no means all, have commas for the first two question marks and an exclamation mark for the last.

Where there are quartos extant of a play, their punctuation may differ so extensively from the Folio that whole passages can be given a different feel. In Hamlet's disquisition on man, modern editors almost invariably follow the syntactic lead in the Folio, which has:

> What a piece of worke is a man! how Noble in Reason? how infinite in faculty? in forme and mouing how expresse and admirable? in Action, how like an Angell? in apprehension, how like a God the beauty of the world, the Parragon of Animals;
> (II ii 304–7)

This reading allows every *how* to have a prepositional phrase dependent upon it because the pattern changes from *how . . . in* to *in . . . how*. It does, nevertheless, leave the last two phrases rather up in the air. One may also notice the question marks where modern editors have exclamation marks. The Second Quarto has a rather different reading:

> What peece of worke is a man, how noble in reason, how infinit in faculties, in forme and moouing, how expresse and admirable in action, how like an Angell in apprehension, how like a God: the beautie of the world; the paragon of Annimales;

This punctuation has a long prepositional group in the middle, *in faculties, in forme and moouing*, so that every *how* is followed by a prepositional group beginning with *in*, except the last one. This makes that last phrase *how like a God* stand out as the climax, which is then qualified by reference to the world and the animals. These last two items are thus brought into closer contact with what has gone before. It is a punctuation which produces a convincing and satisfying reading.

Clearly the punctuation is important in indicating the relationship between various clauses. This is even more so in Elizabethan English than now because, as we saw in the last chapter, there was a smaller range of conjunctions and less overt subordination. It is much more typical for a succession of statements to be placed one after the other with the reader trying to establish what the connections between each one are. In the previous quotation from *Hamlet* the last two phrases, *the beauty of the world, the paragon of animals*, may be interpreted as a sentiment referring generally to all that has gone before or as a specific expansion of the immediately preceding phrase. As a clearer example of this unexpressed relationship, consider this sentence from *The Merchant of Venice*: 'This Hebrew will turne Christian, he growes kinde' (I iii 173). These two statements may be regarded as parallel or causal. If the latter, it is possible to make either clause subordinate: because he wants to become a Christian he is growing kind, or because he is growing kind he will become a Christian. Modern editors either keep the Folio's comma or try to make the link between the two clauses more pointed by having a colon, though that does not explain precisely how they read the sentence.

This problem becomes more acute when there are longer passages of apparently parallel, but linked, clauses or when the word order is ambiguous so that the meaning of a single clause may itself depend upon the wider context. The former of these problems is found in the following passage:

Wrath-kindled Gentlemen be rul'd by me:
Let's purge this choller without letting blood:
This we prescribe, though no Physition,
Deepe malice makes too deepe incision,
Forget, forgiue, conclude, and be agreed,
Our Doctors say, This is no time to bleed.
Good Vnckle, let this end where it begun,
Wee'l calme the Duke of Norfolke; you, your son. (*R2* I i 152–9)

The first two lines end with a colon in the Folio. The colon is usually described as a heavier stop than the semi-colon or as an emphatic pause, though neither description offers any help on how to understand the linking role it plays here. Each line contains a complete clause which could stand independently. Yet the clauses are linked by subject matter and by the theme of blood-letting which runs through them. Modern editors usually replace the first colon with a comma or a semi-colon, though neither seems appropriate. The purging of the anger without letting blood would result from Richard's settling the dispute; the second clause expands the first and so the colon makes reasonable sense. The second colon is normally replaced by a dash in modern editions which suggests that the third line is an expansion of what has gone before. Its *This* is the prescribed remedy. However, the *deepe malice* and the *deepe incision* refer back to the second line, which suggests that perhaps the third line should be understood in parenthesis. Modern editions which have a semi-colon at the end of line three leave the fourth line as a general comment which is only thematically linked with what precedes; it is left suspended in grammatical space. Modern editors keep the full stop at the end of line four, though the suggestions in line five are what are involved in letting Richard rule the disputants. Some editors put a semi-colon after *forgiue*, and most have a colon after *agreed*. The latter implies some relationship between the fifth and sixth lines, though what that is remains uncertain. It could be causal: agree together because doctors say this is no time to bleed; but other interpretations are possible. The full stop at the end of line six is usually kept so that the last two lines are closely linked. Most modern editors put a semi-colon at the end of the penultimate line, though it is rare to find any comment as to what that line means or what its relationship with the following one is. It may well be that Richard means the dispute should end in calmness or peace, which was presumably the state of affairs before the dispute or choler commenced. If so, the final line could explain and expound that idea, for if the two disputants are calmed the previous state of peace will have been restored. If so, a semi-colon does not seem the appropriate mark to use in a modern edition.

The passage consists of eight lines, each of which is an independent unit. It is possible to posit different relationships between these lines and those relationships have to be expressed through the punctuation, since there are no co-ordinating or subordinating conjunctions, and since the linking devices such as *this* are so general they could relate to a variety of referents. A few editors respond to this situation by keeping the Folio punctuation, but that seems inappropriate in a modern spelling edition since the marks meant different things to Shakespeare's printers than they do to us. Unfortunately, the printers used the marks more for declamation than for grammatical clarification, and even then they did not employ the marks in a consistent manner. It is therefore impossible to decide how Shakespeare may have meant these lines to be understood. Their general sense is clear, but their precise grammatical relationship is not. Modern punctuation will inevitably suggest that one particular meaning is correct, for to us punctuation marks have a more logical and grammatical significance. Students should remember, though, that this certainty of meaning is often an editorial intervention; Shakespeare may have been more satisfied with a rather wider range of meaning, as may be true of his use of words – a subject discussed in an earlier chapter. Certainly Shakespeare's own punctuation is thought to have been light. One final point may be made in reference to this type of sentence arrangement. It is unusual to find it in formal, written language today, though it occurs commonly enough at a spoken level. An utterance like 'Be quiet, someone's coming' would be quite normal in less formal language. It should not be assumed from this that by using this method of sentence arrangement, Shakespeare was trying to write colloquially or informally. It was simply that what we consider the more formal variety had yet to be developed in English.

The quartos and Folio do not necessarily agree in what punctuation to employ between clauses, as if Shakespeare's contemporaries were uncertain of what meaning to suggest. These variations can also affect the force of some statements. When Mowbray says:

> now no way can I stray,
> Saue backe to England, all the worlds my way (*R2* I iii 206–7)

the early quartos omit the comma in the middle of the second line. With the comma the phrase *Saue backe to England* can be understood either with what goes before or with what goes afterwards; without it that phrase must be taken with the other half of the line. The former interpretation, which could be understood as 'Now wherever I go I shall not be straying unless I go to England; the whole world is now my road', is somewhat crisper than its alternative because the sentiment concludes with a short pithy generalisation so typical of this play. Although that may be so, it does not necessarily mean it is what Shakespeare intended.

Ellipsis is another common phenomenon in Shakespearian plays, for it helped to bring about the compression and pithiness which was so beloved of Elizabethans. Almost any part of speech may be omitted. When an unusual word order is also involved, it is difficult to know whether one is dealing with ellipsis or a novel construction. Inevitably too some ambiguity may result from the compressed utterances. When Cordelia says 'I returne those duties backe as are right fit' (*Lear* I i 95–6), the compression in the second half of the sentence makes several shades of interpretation possible, though the general meaning is clear. The use of participles and the absence of conjunctions may, as we have seen, aid brevity, though they can lead to problems of interpretation. When Polixenes says:

> Had we pursu'd that life,
> And our weake Spirits ne're been higher rear'd
> With stronger blood, we should haue answer'd Heauen
> Boldly, not guilty; the Imposition clear'd,
> Hereditarie ours (*WT* I ii 71–5)

the last phrase need not actually be an example of ellipsis which implies something is missing grammatically, although much has to be understood to make sense of it. That sense may be 'provided that the guilt of original sin which is ours through birth had been removed'. Some examples of what have been claimed as ellipsis are probably nothing of the sort. Thus Abbot suggests that *bid* has to be understood from *forbid* in the following passage:[2]

> You may as well forbid the Mountaine Pines
> To wagge their high tops, and to make no noise
> When they are fretted with the gusts of heauen.
> (*Merch.* IV i 75–7)

Yet this is simply an example of a double negative in the second phrase dependent upon *forbid*; for the *no* we would today use *any*.

Ellipsis may naturally make it difficult to decide what kind of clause is involved, for in speech the clause would be revealed by the stress and tone adopted by the speaker. Thus when we get an exchange like this one:

LEO.: *Hermione* (my dearest) thou neuer spoak'st
To better purpose.
HER.: Neuer? (*WT* I ii 88–9)

it is possible to assume that Hermione's reply is either a question or an exclamation because in the Folio a question mark can do duty for an exclamation mark. Although Hermione's *Neuer?* is usually kept as a question in modern editions, Hamlet's 'Murther?' (I v 26) in reply to the ghost's use of the same word is more normally edited today as an exclamation. In *Hamlet* there are of course earlier quartos, and these may often have another punctuation, which conveys a different tone from what is said. When Horatio and Marcellus catch up with Hamlet after the ghost's departure, he asks them to grant him one small request. Modern editors here usually follow the Folio reading for Horatio's answer which is 'What is't my Lord? we will' (I v 143). Although the First Quarto has in the place only 'What i'st my Lord?', the Second Quarto has the same reading as the Folio with another punctuation, namely 'What i'st my Lord, we will.' There is no question mark and so Horatio's answer means 'Whatever request you make, we will agree to it'. This is a satisfactory reply and suggests an assurance and solidity not found in the rather more breathless reply which is a question. The reading adopted in an edition may affect our attitude towards Horatio.

There are three types of sentence, declarative or statement, interrogative or question, and imperative or command. These three types are normally distinguished in modern English through their structure, though it is possible to make a statement into a question by altering the tonal pattern, as in 'He is coming?' The ability to make a statement into a question was equally found in Elizabethan English, though the use of the question mark also as an exclamation mark makes it difficult to decide how particular sentences should be understood. Modern editors follow the folio in the following dialogue:

HER.: You'le stay?
POL.: No, Madame.
HER.: Nay, but you will?
POL.: I may not verely. (*WT* I ii 44–5)

Hermione's questions, particularly the latter, could as easily be interpreted as statements verging on commands, though such a reading would perhaps make Hermione more assertive than many critics would prefer. On the other hand, occasionally no question mark is found in the Folio after what seems to be a declarative sentence, though in some cases a question might make better sense. This is true in:

HER.: That's true enough,
Though 'tis a saying (Sir) not due to me.
LEO.: You will not owne it.
HER.: More then Mistresse of,
Which comes to me in name of Fault, I must not
At all acknowledge. (*WT* III ii 55–9)

Here Hermione's latter sentence seems to be a reply to a question and so a question mark after Leontes's *You will not owne it* would seem both possible and appropriate. As has already been noted, the Folio in its punctuation does not necessarily reflect Shakespeare's intentions.

This problem of deciding which type of sentence is meant is compounded by the fact that the structures of these sentence types were not as clearly distinguished in Shakespearian times as they now are. The imperative sentence normally contained the subject, which is today rarely found. Instead of a simple *Come*, Elizabethan English preferred the form *Come you*. Although there are enough unambiguous forms to show that this was common, some examples can be interpreted as a verb followed by a form of address. In *Hamlet* the ghost's 'Know thou Noble youth' (I v 38) is often interpreted by editors as *Know, thou Noble youth*, though it is more probably to be understood as *Know thou, Noble youth.* Interrogatives are not frequently formed with the *do* auxiliary, which is obligatory today, so that *Come you* could as readily be the structure of a question as of a command. Leonato's 'Well then, goe you into hell' (*Ado* II i 35) is perhaps a command as the absence of a question mark in the Folio suggests, though modern editors usually take it to be an interrogative. Questions also frequently have a *wh-* word like *why* or *what* to introduce them, even though those words may be outside the formal structure of the interrogative. Examples like 'What shall this speech be spoke for our excuse?' (*RJ* I iv 1) make this clear; and *why* can of course occur as an indicator of an exclamation in non-interrogative sentences like 'Why 'tis the rarest argument of wonder' (*AW* II iii 7). These words may cause ambiguity at times. When Hector says 'What art thou Greek?' (*Troil.* V iv 25), his words can be understood as *What, art thou Greek?* or *What art thou, Greek?* Indeed the *Greek* could be regarded as the vocative of the next question he utters.

It is important to look at the different types of sentence that go to make up any scene, for that may be a significant feature of its tone and emotion.[3] A series of questions will often indicate urgency in a particular situation, though it can also be used for clowning and wit. The openings of scenes often show a high proportion of questions not simply because they elicit information, but also because they are activating stimuli which help to set the action in motion. However, questions in Shakespeare are much less rarely answered by a simple yes or no as is more characteristic today, for they convey information and act rather in the nature of exclamations. Hence many questions may be answered by another question or by some information which seems not to have much relevance to the question as it is asked. This information may be in the nature of an explanation, although it is not a direct answer to the question. In the following exchange:

QU.: Shall I go win my daughter to thy will?
RICH.: And be a happy Mother by the deed (*R3* IV iv 426–7)

Richard's reply answers the question obliquely and makes the Queen's words almost into an assertion. Ambiguous answers which may be interpreted in several ways are characteristic of comic scenes and in general questions are more frequent in comedies than elsewhere. Some of the tragedies also have a high proportion of questions, which often reflect the probing of motives and attitudes in an attempt to come to terms with a given situation. They are frequent in *Hamlet*, *King Lear* and *Macbeth*. Questions are, however, relatively less frequent in the history plays because they are rather more rhetorical in their presentation and exposition of what happened in the reigns of certain kings. The comedies have shorter sentences with frequent repartee, for which the question is a suitable vehicle. Only *A Midsummer Night's Dream* has few questions and that seems to be the result of its plot. It is a romance suitable to celebrate a wedding, and the play creates a dream-like atmosphere to which scenes of verbal ingenuity would be inappropriate.

There can be no doubt that examination of verbal moods and sentence types can yield important information about the characters in a play. It has been noted that Falstaff uses many conditional sentences introduced by *if* or similar words.[4] Such utterances as 'I am a Rogue if I drunke to day' (*1H4* II iv 145) are frequent on Falstaff's lips. In many such oaths as this Falstaff is damned out of his own mouth, because the audience has just seen him drink. Such statements help to build up his character. He makes outrageous statements which are usually qualified, though the audience know that the qualification is fallacious. It is not possible here to elaborate further on these different constructions; it must suffice to point out that they can be significant.

8 Conclusion

To study the language of a Shakespearian play means looking at many points of detail as well as the linguistic structure and background in the Elizabethan period. It should not be assumed that study of this kind will challenge accepted interpretations of a play, though naturally understanding some utterances correctly or even realising the possible interpretations which an utterance may have could affect our response to the tone of a scene or the make-up of a character. In general in the study of Shakespeare his language has been neglected by readers and editors. The efforts which the latter have put into understanding the typographical and bibliographical details of their texts have not been matched by any attempt to understand the language so that often linguistic emendations are made which seem unnecessary. However, it has to be admitted that there are limits to our understanding of the language, which may indeed have more than one possible interpretation. Generally the language contained more euphony and variety and less subordination than ours. It also had a different structure with fewer grammatical words. This aspect of the language is often overlooked because we attach more importance to meaning and vocabulary.

A problem in interpreting Shakespeare's language is that its surface meaning may not be as logical and grammatical as we expect language to be. Shakespeare and his contemporaries were carried away by sound and theme to the detriment of grammatical sense. Because there were fewer grammatical words, those that did exist tended to carry a greater burden of meaning which makes the elucidation of many passages ambiguous. The difference in structure is found in most aspects of language but is particularly marked in the nominal group. Although some of Shakespeare's structures may be attributed to his poetic flair, the majority are shared by his contemporaries and form the common organisation of the language of the period.

During the course of the book examples have been chosen from various Shakespearian plays to exemplify various linguistic features. It is appropriate to consider now a single passage to give a more rounded view of the language. I have chosen the second scene in Act One of *Troilus and Cressida.* There were clearly difficulties in printing this play in the Folio, for it was finally printed in a different place from that in which it was meant to go. Only two pages are numbered and they are not in the correct sequence. However, these publishing difficulties probably had little implication for the language, for the play was published in a quarto in 1609; the differences between the quarto and folio texts are not great. The scene I shall consider is too long to quote in full, but it contains both prose and poetry. The final lines uttered as a soliloquy by Cressida are worth looking at in detail:

Words, vowes, gifts, teares, & loues full sacrifice,
275 He offers in anothers enterprise:
But more in *Troylus* thousand fold I see,
Then in the glasse of *Pandar*'s praise may be;
Yet hold I off. Women are Angels wooing,
Things won are done, ioyes soule lyes in the dooing:
280 That she belou'd, knowes nought, that knowes not this;
Men prize the thing vngain'd, more then it is.
That she was neuer yet, that euer knew
Loue got so sweet, as when desire did sue:
Therefore this maxime out of loue I teach;
285 *Atchieuement, is command; vngain'd, beseech.*
That though my hearts Contents firme loue doth beare,
Nothing of that shall from mine eyes appeare. (ll. 274–87)

It may be noted immediately that there are some differences between the two texts, for in the penultimate line the Quarto has *Then* for *That* and *content* for *Contents.* The Quarto readings are accepted by most editors, for the first makes easier sense and the second provides a different subject for *doth beare*, which demands a singular noun.

There are also differences in punctuation and these may affect the cohesion across the various clauses. Where the Folio has a colon after *dooing* (l. 279) and a semi-colon after *this* (l. 280), the Quarto has a full-stop and a comma respectively. In the former the *this* appears to refer back to the previous couplet; in the latter it refers forward to the next line. In the middle of line 278 the Folio has a full-stop after *off*, whereas the Quarto has a colon. The Quarto punctuation suggests that the aphorism about the position of women when they are wooed is linked causally with Cressida's policy to maintain a distance from Troilus; it consequently implies coquetry. The Folio punctuation allows her *Yet hold I off* to be linked with her praise of Troilus and so implies more genuine hesitation than feminine strategy. The Folio reading is more often followed by modern editors.

The speech is notable for its balance and repetition, though these features recur throughout the whole scene. It often seems that the rhetorical arrangement is more important than the precise sense, though the use of couplets encourages compression and parallelism. Nevertheless the general sense of the passage is clear, though it might be argued whether it is too wordy in its presentation despite the compression. The language of the play has indeed often been criticised for its playing with words for little apparent purpose. The predominant feature of the language in the speech is the use of participles and generalised subjects like *women, men, she, love* and *atchieuement*. These contribute to that sense of the pithy utterance of proverbial statement, as though Cressida were expressing self-evident truths. Such expressions help to distance her own predicament from the immediate attention of the audience. There is also considerable rhetorical artistry in the lines; in *That she belou'd, knowes nought, that knowes not this* there is repetition of *knowes nought* and *knowes not* with the contrast of *That* at the beginning and *this* at the end of the line.

The nominal group is reasonably simple throughout, with most problems coming from the use of the participle. The use of *she* as the head of a nominal group in *That she belou'd* can create difficulties for a modern reader who would instinctively want to understand this group in a different way. The participle is used as a qualifier so that the group means 'that woman who is loved'. Similar qualifiers are found in *Things won* and *the thing vngain'd*, but the *wooing* in *Angels wooing* is to be taken in a passive sense, as we saw in an earlier chapter. The most problematical line is *Atchieuement, is command; vngain'd, beseech*. The *Atchieuement* refers back to *the thing vngain'd*, which is paralleled by *vngain'd* later in the line, and it must mean 'what has been gained or won', like *Things won* earlier. So the first half means 'What has been won is liable to be commanded (by the captor)'. The *vngain'd* following is a participle which normally in this speech acts as a qualifier but here is acting as head with the sense 'what has not been won'. The final word looks like a verb, but as the two halves of the line are balanced against each other it might be understood as a noun functionally shifted from a verb, for the parallelism suggests a reading *vngain'd is beseech.* The sense must be 'What has not been won is liable to be subjected to the beseechings (of the would-be captor)'. The vocabulary is notably sparse and what difficulty there is in the passage comes from the syntax. Even that is not too difficult when one understands the reliance upon participles in the qualifier position; hence *loue got* means no more than 'love which has been obtained' by one lover yielding to the importunity of the other.

The verbal group is equally straightforward, though the implication of some verbal groups is ambiguous. When line 277 ends *may be*, it is possible to understand it to mean either 'may be seen' or 'could possibly exist'. The latter seems to be correct and is far more critical of Pandarus, for it suggests that Pandarus's mirror is not capable of reflecting Troilus's true worth because Pandarus cannot understand it. He sees only the superficial qualities; Cressida, however, can see into the essence of Troilus. The verb 'to know' changes its meaning in the speech, for in line 280 it means 'understand', but in line 282 it means 'experience'. The sense of lines 280–1 is 'There has never existed a woman for whom love after capitulation to a man was as sweet as the experience of being keenly pursued by a man in love'. The use of the past *did sue* where most other verbs are in the present implies that this experience is a thing of the past and cannot be regained. Its passing is emphasised by the use of *did.* Although there are no passives in the passage the use of abstract subjects like *desire* help to give it the same distancing effect of established opinion which the passive would create in Modern English. The use of *doth* in the penultimate line reinforces the word *firme* and together they create the impression of genuine and unshakeable love. The two ideas which run through the verbs and participles are those of seeing and those of conquest.

There is an ambiguity in the *out of loue* (l. 284), which modern readers might understand to mean from Cressida's own experience of love. It is more likely to mean simply 'concerning love' with the *out of* having much the same meaning as Latin *de.* Cressida is not telling what she has experienced, but what she understands received opinion to be on the subject. Her love for and admiration of Troilus are genuine, even though she is hesitant to declare it. This final speech puts a different gloss on what comes earlier in the scene, where she had seemed pert and playful. There she had used verbal play as a cloak for her true feelings.

Although the majority of the earlier part of the scene is written in prose, it has a high element of parallelism and wordplay. The parallelism is often emphasised through ellipsis as when Cressida's man says 'hee is a gowtie *Briareus*, many hands and no vse; or purblinded *Argus*, all eyes and no sight' (ll. 28–9). Here the qualifying phrases are highly elliptical, for the first means something like 'who has many hands, none of which are usable', and they are only loosely attached grammatically to their head in the nominal group. Parallelism also occurs through the wordplay, for one character may repeat, even if not precisely, what another has said. Pandarus himself delights in repetition, as his opening words show: 'What's that? what's that?' (l. 39). This trick of his makes one wonder whether certain phrases should be taken as repetitive, as when he says 'Paris? Paris is durt to him' (l. 230), which might perhaps be punctuated *Paris, Paris is durt to him.* This echoic tendency may account for the use of the relatively infrequent word *drayman*, for to Cressida's statement about 'Achilles, a better man' Pandarus responds with 'Achilles? a Dray-man' (ll. 240–1).

Because of the quibbling we find fewer Latinate words than we might otherwise expect and there are naturally many questions. It is not always easy to decide precisely what constitutes a question, and editors differ. The Folio prints the following exchange in this way:

PAN.: Was *Hector* arm'd and gon ere yea came to Illium? *Hellen* was not vp? was she?
CRE.: *Hector* was gone but *Hellen* was not vp?
PAN.: E'ene so; *Hector* was stirring early. (45–9)

Cressida's answer is printed as a question in the Quarto too, but the question mark was deleted in the second folio and is not found in subsequent editions. Usually modern editors put a heavy stop after *gone*, understanding her answer to contain two declarative statements. However, since both the earliest texts contain a question mark, we must consider the possibility whether Cressida's words form a question which teasingly mimicks the questions which Pandarus has just asked. Pandarus's *E'ene so* would then be an answer to that question. Such a playful question might be more in the nature of the scene, and to interpret the lines in this way may make them a little more lively than they otherwise are. Several other question marks in the scene stand for exclamations, though again editors are not agreed as to which these are. When Cressida says of Troilus 'Oh he smiles valiantly,' Pandarus's reply 'Dooes hee not?' (ll. 118–19) is more in the nature of a tag and might be better edited without the question mark today.

The punctuation in modern editions often departs unnecessarily from that of the Folio and Quarto. When Cressida's man says of Hector's wrath 'The noise goe's this' (l. 12), many modern editors insert a comma after *goe's.* Yet *this* and *thus* often interchange in Shakespearian texts, though *this* could readily be taken as elliptical for 'in this way'. A comma is unnecessary and breaks up the flow of the line. In a later exchange the Folio has:

PAN.: No not *Hector* is not *Troylus* in some degrees.
CRE.: 'Tis iust, to each of them he is himselfe.
PAN.: Himselfe? alas poore *Troylus* I would he were.
CRE.: So he is. (67–70)

The punctuation in the Quarto is the same except for the omission of the question mark after *Himselfe.* Modern editors put a heavy stop after *them* in Cressida's first speech and after *Troylus* in the following speech by Pandarus. This modern punctuation undermines some of the wordplay. Cressida's first speech means 'Exactly (i.e. that Hector is not Troilus), because each of them is himself (i.e. Hector is Hector and Troilus is Troilus).' Pandarus's reply means 'I could wish that poor Troilus were himself', and the Quarto's punctuation is therefore preferable. Pandarus is taking 'to be oneself' in a different way from Cressida, of course, and what is important in his words is that the *poore Troylus* and *he were* should not be separated by a heavy stop. For Cressida turns what he says round and says 'Indeed he is', implying that Troilus is indeed a poor fellow. The two speakers are here almost carrying on separate monologues, though taking up words uttered by the other in a sense which was not intended.

A further difficulty in editing occurs when Pandarus reminds Cressida that he had informed her of something yesterday, namely that Troilus was in love with her. His next speech goes in Quarto and Folio 'Ile be sworne 'tis true, he will weepe you an 'twere a man borne in Aprill' (ll. 167–8), to which Cressida appropriately replies 'And Ile spring vp in his teares, an 'twere a nettle against May'.

Pandarus's speech is edited today with a heavy stop after *true*, thus making him affirm as truthful his statement about Troilus's love for Cressida. This punctuation implies that he then launches into an elaboration of Troilus's great passion. However, this example of Troilus's love is highly fanciful in the manner of the Elizabethan sonneteers. This fanciful statement needs to be reinforced by an oath to emphasise its veracity and so it is better to take *Ile be sworne 'tis true* to refer to this statement, as is suggested by the punctuation in the Folio and Quarto. It underlines Pandarus's courtly nature, for in swearing that Troilus will weep buckets of tears for Cressida he shows that he knows the rules of the game of love, which is for him a game. His oath underlines the exaggeration and thus elicits Cressida's punning response.

Because the main part of the scene is built around wordplay, there is more emphasis on verbal items than usual. However, we may note the interchange of tenses in the account of Hector's anger by Cressida's man (ll. 3–11), in which the switch from the preterite to the present helps to make that anger seem more immediate and creates dramatic interest. The use of the auxiliary *do* in questions by Pandarus as in his 'do you know a man if you see him?' (l. 63) gives them a slightly fussy and emphatic tone, which tells us something of Pandarus. It is also interesting to contrast his statements 'I thinke he went not forth to day' (l. 212) and 'I doubt he bee hurt' (l. 268). The latter uses the subjunctive after *doubt*, as is usual, though it implies that Pandarus is not convinced that Troilus is hurt. He wishes to suggest to Cressida that he may be without frightening her by suggesting that he really is wounded, On the other hand, his former statement uses no compound verb form in the subordinate clause which therefore has a more definite air, for he is saying 'I am certain that Troilus did not go to the field today'. His words do not imply hesitation, but rather confident assertion.

These and other features of language can be detected in this scene, which I have chosen at random to illustrate what features may be found. A knowledge of the language makes us look more closely at many utterances. It also helps prevent misunderstanding of what Shakespeare wrote, the easiest aspect of which is to read his words as though they were Modern English. We owe it to Shakespeare to understand what his words mean or what are the limits of their understanding before embarking on critical analysis.

Notes

INTRODUCTION

1. J. Milroy, *The Language of Gerard Manley Hopkins* (London: Deutsch, 1977) p. 39.

2. *Cf.* 'If I read a book [and] it makes my whole body so cold no fire ever can warm me I *know* that is poetry. If I feel physically as if the top of my head were taken off, I know *that* is poetry. These are the only way I know it. Is there any other way?' (Emily Dickinson in a letter to Thomas Higginson) see T. H. Johnson and T. Ward, *The Letters of Emily Dickinson* (Cambridge, Mass.: Harvard University Press, 1958) vol. II, pp. 473–4.

3. J. Culler, *Structuralist Poetics* (London: Routledge & Kegan Paul, 1975) ch. 8.

4. For an interesting critique of new readings see R. Levin, *New Readings vs. Old Plays* (Chicago and London: University of Chicago Press, 1979).

2 VARIETIES

1. See for example Dolores M. Burton, *Shakespeare's Grammatical Style* (Austin and London: University of Texas Press, 1973).

2. K. Muir, 'Shakespeare and Rhetoric', *Shakespeare Jahrbuch* 90 (1964) 60; and Kenneth Hudson, 'Shakespeare's use of Colloquial Language', *SS* 23 (1970) 39–48.

3. A. R. Humphreys (ed.), *The First Part of King Henry IV*, 6th edn (London: Methuen, 1966) p. 37.

4. P. J. Gillett, 'Me, U, and Non-U: Class Connotations of Two Shakespearean Idioms', *Shakespeare Quarterly*, 25 (1974) 297–309.

3 VOCABULARY

1. K. Muir (ed.), *King Lear*, 9th edn (London: Methuen, 1972) p. 133.

2. V. Salmon, 'Some Functions of Shakespearean Word-Formation', *SS* 23 (1970) 13–26.

3. Hilda M. Hulme, *Explorations in Shakespeare's Language* (London: Longman, 1962).

4. Richard Farmer, 'Essay on the Learning of Shakespeare', in D. Nichol

Smith *Eighteenth Century Essays on Shakespeare* (Glasgow: MacLehose, 1903) p. 173.

5. Quoted in T. J. B. Spencer (ed.), *Shakespeare's Plutarch* (Harmondsworth: Penguin Books, 1964) p. 201.

6. P. A. Jørgensen, *Redeeming Shakespeare's Words* (Berkeley and London: University of California Press, 1962).

7. Another passage (*1H6* II v 10ff.) is analysed by R. Quirk, in 'Shakespeare and the English Language' in his *The Linguist and the English Language* (London: Arnold, 1974) pp. 61–2.

4 THE NOMINAL GROUP

1. The grammatical terms employed are those particularly associated with systemic grammar, but the majority are found in most modern grammars other than those based on a transformational generative model. See, for example, R. Quirk *et al.*, *A Grammar of Contemporary English* (London: Longman, 1972), and M. Berry, *Introduction to Systemic Linguistics*, 2 vols (London: Batsford, 1975–7).

2. J. M. Lothian and T. W. Craik, *Twelfth Night*, 2nd edn (London: Methuen, 1975) p. 10 " 'Mellow' is an adj., not a transitive vb. (as might be supposed from F's punctuation)."

3. M. R. Ridley, *Antony and Cleopatra* (London: Methuen, 1954) pp. 61–2, see note to II ii 232.

4. Lothian and Craik, *Twelfth Night* p. 71, see note to II v 171.

5. E. A. Abbott, *A Shakespearian Grammar*, rev. edn (London: Macmillan 1872) §430.

6. E. A. J. Honigmann, *King John*, 4th edn (London: Methuen, 1954) p. 57.

7. Ibid., p. 14.

6 ADVERBS, PREPOSITIONS AND CONJUNCTIONS

1. J. H. P. Pafford, *The Winter's Tale* (London: Methuen, 1963) p. 68, see note to III iii 48–9.

7 WORD ORDER AND SENTENCE TYPES

1. V. Salmon, 'Early Seventeenth-Century Punctuation as a Guide to Sentence-Structure', in her *The Study of Language in 17th-Century England* (Amsterdam: Benjamin, 1979) pp. 47–60. The standard book is P. Simpson, *Shakespearian Punctuation* (Oxford: Clarendon, 1911).

2. Abbott, *A Shakespearian Grammar* § 382.

3. See for example Dolores M. Burton, *Shakespeare's Grammatical Style* (Austin and London: University of Texas Press, 1973); V. Salmon, 'Sentence Structures in Colloquial Shakespearian English', *Transactions of the Philological Society* (1965) 105–40; and Kay Wikberg, *Yes-No Questions and Answers in Shakespeare's Plays. A Study in Text Linguistics* (Åbo: Åbo Akademi, 1975).

4. Burton, *Shakespeare's Grammatical Style* (1973).

Select Bibliography

GENERAL REFERENCE

ABBOTT, E. A. *A Shakespearian Grammar*, rev. edn (London: Macmillan, 1872).

ALEXANDER, P. *William Shakespeare, The Complete Works* (London and Glasgow: Collins, 1951).

BROOK, G. L. *The Language of Shakespeare* (London: Deutsch, 1976).

FRANZ, W. *Die Sprache Shakespeares in Vers und Prosa*, 4th edn of *Shakespeare-Grammatik* (Halle: Niemeyer, 1939).

HINMAN, C. *The Norton Facsimile: The First Folio of Shakespeare* (New York: W. W. Norton; London: Hamlyn, 1968).

McMANAWAY, JAMES G. and ROBERTS, JEANNE A, *A Selective Bibliography of Shakespeare: Editions, Textual Studies, Commentary* (Charlottesville: Virginia University Press, 1975).

ONIONS, C. T. *A Shakespeare Glossary*, 2nd edn with enlarged addenda (Oxford: Clarendon 1953).

SCHMIDT, A. *Shakespeare Lexicon*, 3rd edn rev. by G. Sarrazin, 2 vols (New York: Bloom, 1936).

SPEVACK, M. *A Complete and Systematic Concordance to the Works of Shakespeare*, 8 vols (Hildesheim: Olms, 1968–75).

WELLS, S. *Shakespeare: Select Bibliographical Guides* (London: Oxford University Press, 1973).

STUDIES

BALDWIN, THOMAS W. *William Shakespeare's Small Latine & Lesse Greeke*, 2 vols (Urbana: University of Illinois Press, 1944).

BLAND, D. S. 'Shakespeare and the "Ordinary" Word', *SS* 4 (1951) 49–55.

BRADBROOK, M. 'Fifty Years of the Criticism of Shakespeare's Style: A Retrospect', *SS* 7 (1954) 1–11.

BYRNE, M. ST CLARE 'The Foundations of Elizabethan Language', *SS* 17 (1964) 223–39.

CARROLL, WILLIAM C. *The Great Feast of Language in 'Love's Labour's Lost'* (Princeton NJ, Guildford: Princeton University Press, 1976).

CHARNEY, MAURICE *Style in 'Hamlet'* (Princeton NJ: Princeton University Press; London: Oxford University Press, 1969).

CORMICAN, L. A. 'Medieval Idiom in Shakespeare', *Scrutiny* 17 (1950–1) 186–202, 298–317.

CUSACK, B. 'Shakespeare and the Tune of the Time', *SS* 23 (1970) 1–12.

DAHL, L. *Nominal Style in the Shakespearean Soliloquy* (Turku: Turun Yliopisto, 1969).

DORAN, M. *Shakespeare's Dramatic Language* (Madison, Wisc. and London: University of Wisconsin Press, 1976).

ELLIS, HERBERT A. *Shakespeare's Lusty Punning in 'Love's Labour's Lost', with Contemporary Analogues* (The Hague: Mouton, 1973).

EVANS, B. I. *The Language of Shakespeare's Plays*, 2nd edn (London: Methuen, 1959).

EWBANK, I-S. 'Hamlet and the Power of Words', *SS* 30 (1977) 85–102.

FRASER, R. A. *Shakespeare's Poetics in Relation to 'King Lear'* (London: Routledge & Kegan Paul, 1962).

GILLETT, P. J. 'Me, U and Non-U: Class Connotations of Two Shakespearean Idioms', *Shakespeare Quarterly* 25 (1974) 297–309.

GOLDSMITH, U. K. 'Words out of a Hat? Alliteration and Assonance in Shakespeare's Sonnets', *JEGP* 49 (1950) 33–48.

GRIVELET, M. 'Shakespeare as "Corrupter of Words" ', *SS* 16 (1963) 70–6.

HART, A. 'Vocabularies of Shakespeare's Plays', *Review of English Studies* 19 (1943) 128–40.

HAWKES, T. *Shakespeare's Talking Animals* (London: Arnold, 1973).

HUDSON, K. 'Shakespeare's Use of Colloquial Language', *SS* 23 (1970) 39–48.

HULME, H. M. 'The Spoken Language and the Dramatic Text: Some Notes on the Interpretation of Shakespeare's Language', *Shakespeare Quarterly* 9 (1958) 379–86.

——— *Explorations in Shakespeare's Language* (London: Longmans, 1962).

——— 'Shakespeare's Language', in J. Sutherland and J. Hurstfield (eds), *Shakespeare's World* (London: Arnold, 1964).

——— *Yours that Read Him: An Introduction to Shakespeare's Language* (London: Ginn, for Shakespeare Workshop, 1972).

HUME, ROBERT D. 'Individuation and Development of Character through Language', *Shakespeare Quarterly* 24 (1973) 280–300.

JOSEPH, SISTER MIRIAM *Shakespeare's Use of the Arts of Language* (New York: Hafner, 1947).

KAKIETEK, P. *Modal Verbs in Shakespeare's English* (Poznan: Universytet im Adama Mickiewicza, 1972).

JØRGENSEN, PAUL A. *Redeeming Shakespeare's Words* (Berkeley, Calif. and London: University of California Press, 1962).

KÖKERITZ, H. *Shakespeare's Pronunciation* (New Haven: Yale University Press, 1953).

——— 'Shakespeare's Use of Dialect', *Transactions of the Yorkshire Dialect Society* 9 (1951–6) 10–25.

McINTOSH, A. '*As You Like It*: A Grammatical Clue to Character', *Review of English Literature* 4 (1963) 68–81.

MAHOOD, M. M. *Shakespeare's Wordplay* (London: Methuen, 1957).

MILLWARD, C. 'Pronominal Case in Shakespearian Imperatives', *Language* 42 (1966) 10–17.

MULHOLLAND, J. ' "Thou" and "You" in Shakespeare: A Study in the Second Person Pronoun', *English Studies* 48 (1967) 34–43.

MUSGROVE, S. 'Thieves' Cant in *King Lear*', *English Studies* 62 (1981) 5–13.

NOWOTTNY, W. M. T. 'Some Aspects of the Style of *King Lear*', *SS* 13 (1960) 49–57.

———— 'Some Features of Shakespeare's Poetic Language Considered in the Light of Quintilian and Thomas Wilson', *Hebrew University Studies in Literature* 4:2 (1976) 125–37.

PARKER, D. 'Verbal Moods in Shakespeare's Sonnets', *Modern Language Quarterly* 30 (1969) 331–9.

PARTRIDGE, A. C. *Orthography in Shakespeare and Elizabethan Drama. A Study of Colloquial Contractions, Elision, Prosody and Punctuation* (London: Arnold, 1964).

———— *The Language of Renaissance Poetry* (London: Deutsch, 1971).

QUIRK, R. 'Shakespeare and the English Language', in K. Muir and S. Schoenbaum (eds), *A New Companion to Shakespeare Studies* (London: Cambridge University Press, 1971) pp. 67–82.

RANSOM, JOHN CROW 'On Shakespeare's Language', *Sewanee Review* 55 (1948) 181–98.

SALMON, V. 'Sentence Structures in Colloquial Shakespearian English', *Transactions of the Philological Society* (1965) 105–40.

———— 'Elizabethan Colloquial English in the Falstaff Plays', *Leeds Studies in English* n.s. 1 (1967) 37–70.

———— 'Early Seventeenth-Century Punctuation as a Guide to Sentence Structure', in her *The Study of Language in 17th-Century England* (Amsterdam: Benjamin, 1979) 47–60.

SCHÄFER, J. *Shakespeares Stil: germanisches und romanisches Vokabular* (Frankfurt: Athenäum, 1973).

SIMPSON, P. *Shakespearian Punctuation* (Oxford: Clarendon, 1911).

VICKERS, B. *The Artistry of Shakespeare's Prose* (London: Methuen, 1968).

WIKBERG, K. *Yes-No Questions and Answers in Shakespeare's Plays. A Study in Text Linguistics*, Acta Academiae Aboensis: A Humaniora 51: 1 (Åbo: Åbo Akademi, 1975).

WILLCOCK, G. D. *Shakespeare as Critic of Language* (London: Oxford University Press, for Shakespeare Association, 1934).

———— 'Shakespeare and Rhetoric', *Essays and Studies* 29 (1943) 50–61.

———— 'Shakespeare and Elizabethan English', *SS* 7 (1954) 12–24.

WILSON, F. P. 'Shakespeare and the Diction of Common Life', *Proceedings of the British Academy* 27 (1941) 167–97.

Table of Passages Quoted

In the alphabetical arrangement the articles are disregarded; the historical plays are listed under the names of the kings; and the poetic texts come at the end.

	Act	*Scene*	*Line*	*Page*
All's Well that Ends Well	II	i	55–6	114
	II	i	188–9	102
	II	iii	7	129
	V	iii	176–7	6
Antony and Cleopatra	I	iii	35–6	60
	I	iii	69–71	61
	I	iii	99–101	61
	I	v	43	68
	I	v	70–2	53
	II	i	20–2	62
	II	ii	171	60
	II	ii	181–2	68
	II	ii	195–209	49
	II	ii	232	54
	II	ii	236	58
	II	iii	21	67
	II	iv	1–2	112
	II	v	21	54
	II	vi	16	63
	II	vi	59	101
	II	vii	122–3	52
	III	i	1	52
	III	xii	22	108

	Act	*Scene*	*Line*	*Page*
Love's Labour's Lost	IV	ii	53	41
	IV	iii	163–6	99
	V	i	78	25
	V	ii	908	108
Macbeth	I	vii	1–2	90
	I	vii	2–5	116
	II	i	5	79
	II	ii	37–40	57
	II	ii	62	25
	III	iv	120–1	85
	III	iv	136–8	98
	III	vi	41	36
	IV	ii	66	88
	IV	ii	69	100
	V	i	70–1	95
	V	ii	3	77
	V	v	31–2	96
	V	viii	12–13	93
Measure for Measure	II	ii	5–6	100
	II	ii	17	2
	II	ii	52–3	91
	IV	ii	33	37
The Merchant of Venice	I	ii	22–3	110
	I	iii	7	91
	I	iii	173	123
	II	i	17–20	87
	II	ii	1–17	29–30
	II	iv	39	93
	II	vi	40	93
	II	viii	25–6	93
	III	i	72	75
	III	ii	61	88
	IV	i	75–7	126
	V	i	237	26
The Merry Wives of Windsor	I	i	196	52

	Act	Scene	Line	Page
Cont.:	IV	i	125–9	114
	V	i	90	77
	V	ii	41–3	115
	V	iii	52	98
Richard III	I	iii	348	98
	II	iii	27–30	115
	II	iii	39	109
	III	ii	99	99
	III	v	35	109
	III	v	56–7	101
	IV	ii	60–1	104
	IV	iv	190–5	89
	IV	iv	267–9	113
	IV	iv	426–7	129
	IV	iv	440	86
Romeo and Juliet	I	i	174–8	68
	I	iv	1	128
	I	v	9–10	98
The Taming of the Shrew	I	i	3	97
	I	ii	5–14	36
	III	ii	194–6	91
	IV	iv	15–16	111
The Tempest	I	ii	387	95
	II	ii	15	114
	II	ii	63	95
	II	ii	70	112
	III	ii	50–2	86
	IV	i	26–7	90
	IV	i	122–4	118
	V	i	118–19	89
Timon of Athens	I	i	140–2	106
	II	ii	156	27
	IV	iii	23	51
	V	i	179–80	111

SHENANDOAH UNIVERSITY LIBRARY
WINCHESTER, VA 22601